MW00610368

COMBAT AIRCRAFT

153 KAWANISHI H6K 'MAVIS' AND H8K 'EMILY' UNITS

SERIES EDITOR TONY HOLMES

153 COMBAT AIRCRAFT

Edward M Young

KAWANISHI H6K 'MAVIS' AND H8K 'EMILY' UNITS

OSPREY
PUBLISHING

OSPREY PUBLISHING
Bloomsbury Publishing Plc
Kemp House, Chawley Park, Cumnor Hill, Oxford OX2 9PH, UK
29 Earlsfort Terrace, Dublin 2, Ireland
1385 Broadway, 5th Floor, New York, NY 10018, USA
E-mail: info@ospreypublishing.com
www.ospreypublishing.com

OSPREY is a trademark of Osprey Publishing Ltd

First published in Great Britain in 2024

© Osprey Publishing Ltd, 2024

All rights reserved. No part of this publication may be reproduced or transmitted
in any form or by any means, electronic or mechanical, including photocopying,
recording, or any information storage or retrieval system, without prior
permission in writing from the publishers.

A catalogue record for this book is available from the British Library.

ISBN: PB 9781472860620; eBook 9781472860613; ePDF 9781472860644;
XML 9781472860637

24 25 26 27 28 10 9 8 7 6 5 4 3 2 1

Edited by Tony Holmes
Cover Artwork by Gareth Hector
Aircraft Profiles by Jim Laurier
Index by Alison Worthington
Typeset by PDQ Digital Media Solutions, UK
Printed and bound in India by Replika Press Private Ltd

Osprey Publishing supports the Woodland Trust, the UK's leading woodland
conservation charity.

To find out more about our authors and books visit **www.ospreypublishing.com**.
Here you will find extracts, author interviews, details of forthcoming events and
the option to sign up for our newsletter.

Front Cover

In the spring of 1944, 851st Kokutai
transferred a detachment of H8K2 flying
boats from Southeast Asia to Davao, on
Mindanao, to participate in missions
evacuating key personnel from the Imperial
Navy base at Rabaul to Truk. From Truk,
evacuated personnel went by flying boat to
Saipan and then on to Japan. After
completing these missions in early May,
851st Kokutai received orders to maintain
the detachment at Davao to patrol to the
southwest of the Philippines. During the
invasion of the Marianas the 851st Kokutai
detachment sent four H8K2s to operate out
of Palau. On 2 July 1944, a patrolling US
Navy PB4Y-1 Liberator from VB-115 shot
down an H8K2 from 851st Kokutai
southwest of Palau, likely on its way back to
Davao. There were no survivors from the
flying boat crew (*Cover Artwork by Gareth
Hector*)

Previous Pages

After the end of the war, an H6K4-L
transport sits at the Dai Nippon Kokutai K.K.
base at Yokohama opposite an H8K2
(mostly out of shot). The 'Mavis' has been
repainted in a standard surrender scheme,
consisting of a white finish overall and
green crosses (*GAF_image_804_1,
Museum of Flight (MoF)*)

CONTENTS

INTRODUCTION

The Kawanishi H6K Navy Type 97 Flying Boat ('Mavis') and its successor, the Kawanishi H8K Navy Type 2 Flying Boat ('Emily'), were the principal flying boats of the Imperial Japanese Naval Air Force (IJNAF) during the Pacific War. In action from the first day of the conflict until near the end, they patrolled every stretch of Japan's conquered territory in the Greater East Asian Co-Prosperity Sphere from the Aleutian Islands to the atolls of the Central Pacific, from the Solomon Islands west to the Netherlands East Indies, and beyond to the Andaman Islands in the Indian Ocean.

The IJNAF began the war with just two dedicated flying boat units, the Toko and Yokohama Kokutai (Air Group), adding a third group, 14th Kokutai, in April 1942. These three air groups, re-numbered in the IJNAF's reorganisation in November 1942, continued in action until operational losses and changing strategic demands forced their consolidation into a single air group in early 1945.

The Type 97 Flying Boat had exceptional range, its crews regularly flying ten- to fifteen-hour patrol missions, but its lack of armour protection and self-sealing fuel tanks made the aircraft vulnerable to Allied fighters. During 1943, the Type 97 was progressively withdrawn as Kawanishi increased production of the more capable Type 2 Flying Boat, although the 'Mavis' continued to undertake anti-submarine warfare (ASW) patrols and transport flights.

The Kawanishi Experimental 9-Shi Ogata Hiko Tei prototype. It was later fitted with larger engines and entered service as the H6K1 Type 97 Flying Boat. The IJNAF had Kawanishi develop racks that attached to the wing struts, allowing the flying boat to carry two 800 kg torpedoes (as seen here) or up to twelve 60 kg or 250 kg bombs *(208-03-31_image_509_01, Peter M Bowers Collection, MoF)*

The Type 2 Flying Boat had even greater range than the Type 97, being capable of missions lasting as long as 24 hours covering nearly 4500 statute miles. The Type 2 was the fastest flying boat in service during World War 2. It had armour protection for the crew, self-sealing fuel tanks and a heavy defensive armament of multiple 20 mm gun turrets. Allied pilots treated the Type 2 with respect, but as with the Type 97, the US Navy's carrier fighters would prove to be its nemesis.

The primary mission of the IJNAF's flying boats was reconnaissance. From the earliest days of Japanese naval aviation, the Imperial Japanese Navy (IJN) recognised how important reconnaissance would be to fleet operations and the defence of the Home Islands. As Rear Admiral John McCain, commanding the Aircraft Scouting Force for the US Navy's Atlantic Fleet, commented in early 1942;

'Information is without doubt the most important service required by a fleet commander. Accurate, complete and up to the minute knowledge of the position, strength and movement of enemy forces is very difficult to obtain under war conditions. If these facts are made available while the enemy is at a great distance from our shores and similar information about our own forces is denied the enemy, the commander is given time to plan his movements and select the time and position of contact in such a manner that he may operate under a tactical advantage.'

During the interwar years the IJNAF developed two types of aircraft for aerial reconnaissance. To meet the fleet's immediate needs for reconnaissance, it acquired single-engined floatplanes that could be carried and catapulted from cruisers. These aircraft, such as the Kawanishi E7K1 Type 94 Reconnaissance Seaplane (Allied code name 'Alf') and the later Aichi E13A1 Type 0 Reconnaissance Seaplane (Allied code name 'Jake') had a range of 300–500 miles. For long-range reconnaissance well beyond the fleet, the IJNAF, like the US Navy, relied on the large flying boat.

The challenge for both the Japanese and the American navies was to acquire flying boats that would have the range to sweep the vast stretches of the Pacific Ocean. Historian Edward S Miller described the problem facing the US Navy, and also the IJN, in his essay 'Eyes of the Fleet – How the flying boat transformed War Plan Orange' as follows;

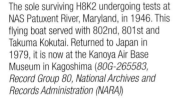

The sole surviving H8K2 undergoing tests at NAS Patuxent River, Maryland, in 1946. This flying boat served with 802nd, 801st and Takuma Kokutai. Returned to Japan in 1979, it is now at the Kanoya Air Base Museum in Kagoshima (*80G-265583, Record Group 80, National Archives and Records Administration (NARA)*)

'The Navy lacked the means of intelligence of enemy naval whereabouts in a theater where island bases were vulnerable to attack from any point of the compass. Security would depend on aircraft that could search a thousand miles in all directions. Such long-range scouts would also be critical for battle operations in the open seas where hostile armadas might close upon each other by 500 miles overnight. The aircraft carrier had introduced the "frightening possibility" of a superior fleet lost through inferior reconnaissance. The side that remained hidden and launched its planes first might destroy the enemy carriers by an "unanswered salvo" and dominate the skies altogether. Victory would depend on the earliest information found by long-range aircraft.'

During the 1920s the IJN came to designate the United States as its main 'hypothetical enemy'. It understood that war with America would involve the westward movement of the US Navy's Pacific Fleet towards Japan, resulting in a decisive naval battle in the Western Pacific. There were four likely approach routes for the Pacific Fleet;

1. A northern route from Pearl Harbor or the American West Coast up along the Aleutian Islands chain to Japan.
2. A southern route via the South Pacific.
3. A central route from Pearl Harbor directly to the Mariana Islands.
4. A central route that went through the Gilbert and Marshall Islands (then the Japanese Mandated Islands) to Truk and on to Guam.

The IJNAF had to have the capacity to patrol all four possible routes to alert Imperial Naval Headquarters to the approach of the Pacific Fleet, and to give the IJN time to prepare for the decisive battle. It would take the IJNAF until the late 1930s to acquire, in the Type 97 Flying Boat, the capability to meet this requirement.

Acknowledgements

In preparing this Osprey book I have used material from the American and British National Archives, selected volumes of the Senshi Sosho (War History) Series relating to the IJNAF in World War 2, the Kodochosho (Mission Reports) for the flying boat units and several Japanese language materials on IJNAF flying boats. I am grateful to Ms Takeda Owada for her excellent translations.

The work of Michael James Claringbould, Peter Ingman and Dr Tom Lewis OAM documenting the air war in the South Pacific was invaluable. I would particularly like to thank Edward Rogers, James Sawruk and Steve Birdsall for alerting me to the clashes between B-17 Flying Fortresses and H6K 'Mavis' flying boats over the Solomons, and for generously sharing the results of their own research into these combats. James Carter of the South Pacific World War 2 Museum kindly sent me information on the Japanese bombing raids on Espiritu Santo.

Photographs for this volume came from several sources. I would like to thank Nicole Davis at the Museum of Flight in Seattle, Washington, Debbie Seracini at the San Diego Air and Space Museum in San Diego, California, Sugiyama Seiko at the Yamato Museum in Kure, Japan, N Hara at ShinMaywa Industries, Ltd, Mainichi Newspapers, the staff of the Still Pictures Branch, Archives II, National Archives and Records Administration at College Park, Maryland, and the staff of the Imperial War Museum in London.

CHAPTER ONE

IJNAF MARITIME PATROL AVIATION 1921–41

The F.5 was the first flying boat to serve with the IJNAF, the Sempill Mission bringing nine examples of the Felixstowe aircraft to Japan. More were acquired from Short Brothers, and it was put into production at the Hiro Kaigun Kosho. Aichi Tokei Denki Kabushiki Kaisha also built 40 F.5s for the IJNAF (*Author's Collection*)

I n the aftermath of World War 1, the IJN realised that its aviation arm had fallen behind developments in the West. The conflict demonstrated that aviation could play a vital role in naval warfare, although its full potential would take time to develop. The war had shown the potential value of flying boats for aerial reconnaissance, ASW patrol and convoy protection.

Noting that the British then led the world in naval aviation, the Japanese government asked the British Foreign Office to send an official naval aviation mission to Japan to establish a flying school and to train naval aviators in the latest combat techniques. Reluctant to send an official mission, the British government agreed to an 'unofficial' mission comprised of men who had served in the Royal Naval Air Service (RNAS) and the Royal Air Force (RAF) during the war, under the leadership of Col Sir William Forbes-Sempill (later Baron Sempill). Arriving in April 1921, the Sempill Mission's experienced staff gave basic flying instruction, trained maintenance personnel and taught combat flying. The Mission brought 113 British aircraft to Japan, including nine Felixstowe F.5 flying boats built by Short Brothers.

Oswald Short led a small team to Japan to work at the IJN's Yokosuka Kaigun Kosho (Naval Arsenal) south of Tokyo erecting the F.5s, with the first flight of a Japanese example taking place on 30 August 1921. Four days later, the F.5 was one of nine aircraft that flew in formation welcoming Crown Prince Michi Hirohito, embarked in an IJN battleship, upon his return from a tour of Europe.

Maj Herbert Brackley, who had flown with the RNAS and the RAF in the war, began training IJNAF pilots on the F.5. Brackley tested a second F.5 in January 1922, and after a third aircraft had been assembled, in early April he led a flight of three F.5s with two Japanese pilots on a long-distance flight around southern Japan, flying from Yokosuka to Sasebo, on the northwest coast of Kyushu, before returning to Yokosuka. In 19 hours and 20 minutes of flying time, the three F.5s covered nearly 1700 miles, stopping at several cities en route. Long-distance flights around Japan became the final test for pilots converting to the F.5.

The IJNAF acquired more F.5 flying boats, purchasing three directly from Short Brothers in 1922. It assigned them to land-based naval air units at Yokosuka and Sasebo, the first two IJNAF bases to be established. The air components had a mixed complement of aircraft, including flying boats and floatplanes.

Both Yokosuka and Sasebo had small naval aircraft factories, but in 1920 the IJNAF established a new factory near the Kure Kaigun Kosho known as the Hiro Kaigun Kosho (Hiro Naval Arsenal). It began building F.5s towards the end of 1921 under licence from Short Brothers with the help of company engineers. The Yokosuka Kaigun Kosho built ten F.5s, with the Hiro Kaigun Kosho delivering an additional ten. To obtain yet more F.5s, the IJNAF contracted with the Aichi Tokei Denki Kabushiki Kaisha (Aichi Watch and Electric Machinery Company, Ltd) to build the flying boat, and the company duly completed 40 by the end of the 1920s. In December 1927 Yokosuka Kokutai had 12 F.5s in service, while Sasebo Kokutai had eight.

As Japanese flying boat pilots gained experience, they undertook more long distance flights. In July 1923 the commanding officer of Yokosuka Kokutai sent two F.5s on a long flight towards the Bonin Islands, the two aircraft covering an estimated 600 nautical miles (690 statute miles) in nine hours. In May 1925, two F.5s made a round trip flight from Yokosuka to Ondomari (now Korsakov), at the southern end of Sakhalin Island, covering 1900 miles in five days.

These two F.5s from Sasebo Kokutai were photographed at their moorings shortly after arriving in Shanghai in 1926 following a flight from Tsingtao. The IJNAF used its flying boats for long flights around Japan, to Korea and to the Bonin Islands. (P20211110dd1dd1phj586000 courtesy Mainichi Newspapers)

The IJNAF replaced the now elderly F.5 with the H1H1 Type 15 Flying Boat from 1929. This H1H1 from Yokosuka Kokutai is being led by a Yokosuka-built Navy Type 14 Reconnaissance Seaplane (E1Y2), also assigned to the Kokutai (*2008-3-31_image_597_01, Peter M Bowers Collection, MoF*)

The Type 15 (H1H1) flying boat served with the IJNAF well into the 1930s, with the later Type 15-2 (H1H3) being assigned to Tateyama Kokutai as shown in this Japanese postcard from 1935 (*Author's Collection*)

A year later two more F.5s from Sasebo Kokutai flew to Shanghai via Mokpo, a port on the southwestern tip of Korea, and Tsingtao (now Qingdao), in China. The flying boats flew directly from Tsingtao to Shanghai, a distance of 340 miles, with the entire flight from Sasebo to Shanghai taking 14 hours. On their return, the F.5s flew directly from Shanghai to Sasebo. On 11 July 1926, two F.5s made the first successful flight from Yokosuka to the Bonin Islands, a distance of 524 miles covered in just under eight hours.

That same year the IJNAF instructed the Hiro Kaigun Kosho to develop a replacement for the F.5. The naval aircraft factory came up with a conventional, improved, wooden biplane design. The prototype, designated the H1H1, was completed in the autumn of 1927 and test flown in March 1928. The IJNAF accepted the H1H1 as the Type 15 Flying Boat, and it went into production at the Hiro and Yokosuka Kaigun Kosho, which built around 20 examples between 1929 and 1932, and at Aichi, which built an additional 45 aircraft between 1929 and 1934. The Type 15s were allocated to the Yokosuka and Sasebo Kokutai, where they established a reputation for reliability.

On 20 May 1929, two Type 15 flying boats flown by Lt Cdr Akira Ito and Lt Nobuzo Susumu took off from Yokosuka for a flight to Saipan, stopping at Chichi Jima, in the Bonin Islands, on the way due to engine trouble. After repairs, they reached Saipan on 22 May. They arrived back in Japan three days later, having covered 2927 miles, making this the IJNAF's longest ocean flight to date. En route to the Bonin Islands during the return flight, aircraft YO51 developed an oil leak in one of its Lorraine

2 engines. PO1c Shuji Sakurai, a mechanic on board, calmly climbed out onto the wing to repair the oil leak, allowing the flying boat to complete the journey to Chichi Jima.

During these years the nascent Japanese aviation industry was reliant on foreign aircraft and engineers for inspiration, but it started incorporating what was learned into local designs of flying boats for the IJNAF. In 1928, a Supermarine Southampton II with an all-metal hull powered by two Napier Lion engines was acquired by the IJNAF. After testing at Yokosuka, the Southampton went to the Hiro Kaigun Kosho for detailed study, with the goal of developing an improved flying boat as a replacement for the Type 15. The result was the H2H1 flying boat that the IJNAF adopted in March 1932 as the Type 89 Flying Boat.

The Type 89 featured an all-metal hull, a fabric-covered all-metal wing and various aerodynamic refinements. Powered by two 550 hp Hiro Type 14 or 600–750 hp Hiro Type 90 12-cylinder liquid-cooled engines, the Type 89 had a maximum speed of 119–122mph – a modest improvement over the Type 15. The Hiro Kaigun Kosho began building Type 89s in 1930, completing 13 aircraft, with Aichi building four from 1931.

To broaden the manufacturing base for flying boats, in early 1928 the IJNAF approached the Aeroplane Department of the Kawanishi Kikai Seisakusho (Kawanishi Machinery Manufacturing Works) to build it aircraft. Up to this time, Kawanishi's Aeroplane Department had only built commercial single-engined mail-carrying aircraft and transport seaplanes, and nothing for the Imperial Japanese Army Air Force (IJAAF) or the IJNAF. In November the Aeroplane Department split off from its parent company and became the Kawanishi Kokuki KK (Kawanishi Aircraft Company), with former IJNAF pilot Cdr Ryohei Arisaka as chief engineer. The IJNAF gave the new company a contract for the Yokosuka-designed Type 13 Seaplane Trainer (K1Y2) and transferred production of the Nakajima Type 15 Reconnaissance Seaplane (E2N1) to Kawanishi.

The IJNAF also contracted Kawanishi to help with production of the Hiro Type 89 Flying Boat so as to give it experience of building flying boats. Shortly thereafter, the IJNAF engaged the company in a significant undertaking when it gave Kawanishi a contract to work with Short Brothers to develop a large, long-range flying boat. With the approval of the British government, Kawanishi sent an engineer to Short Brothers to investigate its latest designs and manufacturing methods.

Kawanishi was interested in the three-engined, all-metal S.8 Calcutta flying boat, but with Rolls-Royce Buzzard engines in place of the Bristol Jupiters that powered the seven aircraft built for Imperial Airways and the six constructed by Short Brothers for the RAF (the latter christened the

Short Brothers designed a new flying boat for the IJNAF designated the KF.1, granting Kawanishi a licence for production in Japan as the Navy Type 90-2 Flying Boat (H3K1). This photograph shows Short Brothers test pilot John Parker flying a KF.1 near the Kawanishi factory at Naruo, near Osaka, in April 1931 (*3B-35307, RG342FH, NARA*)

flying boat Rangoon). The company concurrently developed an enlarged version of the S.8 as the KF.1 and entered into a licence agreement allowing Kawanishi to build the design in Japan. After flight testing in Britain in October 1930, the KF.1 prototype was shipped to Japan along with a team of Short engineers who helped assemble the flying boat at the newly built Kawanishi factory at Naruo, east of Osaka.

The KF.1 was the largest flying boat built in Japan up to that date, with a longer wingspan than the Type 89, more than twice the loaded weight, higher maximum and cruising speeds and a range of 2000 miles. The first Kawanishi-built aircraft flew in March 1932, followed by a second example in November and two more in February 1933. In October 1932 the IJNAF formally accepted the KF.1 as the Navy Type 90-2 Flying Boat (H3K1).

Development of the Type 90-2 took place as the IJN embarked on an expansion of its naval air arm. The London Naval Treaty, signed in April 1930, imposed new restrictions on Japanese naval warship tonnage. As a result, the IJN decided to strengthen areas that the London Treaty did not cover, including aviation. It initiated the first of several 'circle' plans covering naval rearmament. The first two requested funding for new types of aircraft, including a large flying boat, and more land-based and carrier air units.

Between 1930 and 1937, the IJNAF built nine new airfields in the home islands and in Korea. To protect the Tokyo area, it established a new airfield at Tateyama, located at the southern tip of the Chiba Peninsula east of Tokyo Bay, in 1930. Amongst the units established there was a flying boat Chutai (squadron). As they were completed, the new Type 90-2 Flying Boats were assigned to Tateyama, joining several Type 15 flying boats as well as a floatplane and fighter Chutai.

During the early 1930s, the IJNAF had its flying boat units make regular long distance flights around the home islands and to destinations in Korea, Formosa (as Taiwan was then called) and the islands to the south of Japan as part of their annual training. Sasebo Kokutai began the practice of flying from Sasebo to Formosa, completing a flight in the spring of 1930. In April 1931 it undertook the flight with four flying boats to the IJN base at Mako (now Magong), in the Pescadores Islands

In 1930 the Hiro Kaigun Kosho began work on a large, all-metal, three-engined flying boat in the form of the Type 90-1 (H3H1). The first large all-metal aircraft of Japanese design, the Type 90-1 was not a success, although it provided valuable experience for later designs (*Author's Collection*)

off Formosa's west coast. The Sasebo unit made a return flight to Formosa in June 1932. Three months later, the Type 90-2 flying boats conducted their first long-distance flight around the home islands, flying from their base at Tateyama to Sasebo via stops at the northern end of Honshu and on the Honshu west coast, with a direct flight from Sasebo to Tateyama on their return.

Tragically the first Type 90-2 was lost in a crash on 9 February 1933 during a night training exercise, killing Lt Cdr Shinzo Susumu, one of the most experienced flying boat pilots in the IJNAF. Previously, another Type 90-2 had been badly damaged during a typhoon that hit Tateyama in the autumn of 1932, leaving just three examples operational. Tateyama Chutai was active during the summer of 1933, beginning in May when four Type 15 flying boats and two Type 90-2s flew from their base to Chichi Jima, in the Bonin Islands, and returned to Tateyama – a journey of 1010 miles.

In June the three remaining Type 90-2s from Tateyama Chutai flew from Sasebo directly to Keelung on Formosa, covering 1310 miles through adverse weather in eight hours and thirty minutes. Not to be outdone, Sasebo Kokutai sent three Type 15 flying boats to Keelung in May, stopping at Okinawa to refuel. These flights gave crews valuable experience in long-distance, over-water navigation – a critical feature of maritime patrol aviation. They also received wide coverage in the Japanese press.

Although the aircraft's performance was successful and established Kawanishi's reputation as a capable builder of flying boats, the IJNAF considered the Type 90-2 impractical. Instead, it turned again to the Hiro Kaigun Kosho to design a monoplane flying boat to replace the older Types 15 and 89. The Hiro Kaigun Kosho had built a large experimental flying boat, the first Japanese designed large all-metal aircraft, as the Type 90-1 (H3H1). Although it proved to be unsatisfactory as a military aircraft, the experience gained with the Type 90-1 helped the Hiro Kaigun Kosho design the all-metal Type 91 Flying Boat (H4H1),

Once in service, the large Type 90-2 Flying Boat proved impractical. The IJNAF turned to the Hiro Kaigun Kosho for a more suitable aircraft, and it designed the Navy Type 91 Flying Boat (H4H1) as a replacement for the Types 15 and 89. The H4H1, shown here, was powered by two 600 hp Type 91-2 liquid-cooled engines (2008-3-31_image_596_01, Peter M Bowers Collection, MoF)

a twin-engined monoplane with the engines mounted above the wing. Performance proved superior to the Types 15 and 89. Production of the Type 91 began at the Hiro Kaigun Kosho, which built around 30 aircraft, in 1933. The IJNAF also contracted Kawanishi to build 17 Type 91s.

Several limitations with the design soon manifested themselves once the flying boat was in service, and in 1937 the IJNAF decided to cease production. The Type 91s were assigned to Yokosuka Kokutai and Tateyama Chutai, where they began undertaking long-distance training flights. In August 1934 two Type 91 flying boats from Tateyama completed a 12-hour non-stop 1381-mile round-trip flight between Tateyama and Sasebo.

The IJNAF, however, was already looking toward flying boats with performance superior to the Type 91. From 1930 it started thinking about using long-range land-based attack aircraft to strike an advancing American fleet far from Japan, particularly if the IJNAF could base these aircraft on its Mandated Islands in the Central Pacific. The Naval General Staff also recognised that by using these islands, larger flying boats could range far out into the Pacific in search of an enemy fleet. At the same time, then Rear Admiral Isoroku Yamamoto put forward a plan, adopted in 1932, that would require all aircraft and aircraft engines for military use to be designed by Japanese engineers in an effort to boost the capability of the local aviation industry.

In March 1933 the IJNAF awarded Kawanishi an 8-Shi (eighth year of the Showa reign) requirement for a large experimental flying boat. To meet the 8-Shi specification, the company developed two designs for monoplane flying boats – the Type Q, with four planned 1500 hp liquid-cooled engines mounted on a high cantilever wing, and the Type R with three engines. During 1933 Kawanishi engineers tested models of these aircraft in wind tunnels and water tanks to determine their projected performance, but neither design met the IJNAF's expectations. It withdrew the 8-Shi specification, replacing it with an even more demanding set of requirements as the 9-Shi Ogata Hiko Tei (Large Body Flying Boat), awarded exclusively to Kawanishi on 18 January 1934.

The IJNAF wanted a large, four-engined flying boat with performance superior to any American or European aircraft of this type. In March 1934, the Sikorsky S-42 flying boat – the largest heavier-than-air aircraft yet built in America – made its first flight. Developed for Pan American Airways, the S-42 demonstrated exceptional speed and range, with a maximum speed 50 mph greater than the Type 91-1 and more than double its maximum range. The IJNAF required something better, demanding a minimum cruising speed of 120 knots (138 mph) and a range of not less than 2495 nautical miles (2871 statute miles).

In November 1934 Kawanishi began design work on the Type S, as the new model was designated. The prototype emerged from the Kawanishi factory at Naruo in July 1936, making its first flight on 14 July. Eleven days later, Kawanishi handed over the prototype to the IJNAF with a suitable ceremony, including Shinto rites. The new flying boat was a parasol monoplane with a span greater than the S-42 or the newer Martin M-130 Clipper. The all-metal wing, a first for Kawanishi, was mounted to the hull on inverted V-struts, with parallel bracing struts extending

diagonally from the fuselage side to the middle of the wing. Kawanishi added flaps to the wing – another first for Japanese flying boats. Four 840 hp Nakajima Hikari nine-cylinder air-cooled radial engines powered the prototype, which featured three gun positions in tail and dorsal turrets and in an open bow position.

The Type S met all the 9-Shi requirements, although it was considered slightly underpowered. The IJNAF accepted the new flying boat as the Type 97 (H6K1). The initial production series was the Type 97 Model 2 (H6K2), later to be designated the Type 97 Model 11 in 1940. The flying boat had a normal cruising speed of 138 mph, a maximum speed of 206 mph and a range with full combat load of 2230 nautical miles (2566 statute miles) (see *Osprey Duel 126 – H6K "Type 97"/H8K "Emily" vs PB4Y-1/2 Liberator/Privateer* for more details on the development of the H6K).

Impressed with the Type 97's speed and range, the IJNAF added an offensive capability to its new flying boat. Kawanishi equipped it with two hardpoints, one fixed to each set of the diagonal struts supporting the wing, to hold twelve 60 kg or four 250 kg bombs, or two 800 kg torpedoes.

While the Type 97 flying boat was undergoing development, testing and initial production, the IJNAF continued the rapid expansion of its land- and carrier-based air arms. In 1935, a new airfield at Saeki, on the northeast coast of Kyushu, was established to guard the approaches to the IJN's main base at Kure. It sent a half-squadron of H4H1 flying boats to Saeki to patrol the areas south of Kyushu.

More significantly for the history of IJNAF maritime patrol aviation, in October 1936 the first dedicated flying boat unit, Yokohama Kokutai, was established southeast of Tokyo. Prior to this time, as previously noted, IJNAF Kokutai had been composite units, containing mixed squadrons of fighters, attack aircraft, floatplanes and, at Yokosuka, Sasebo, Tateyama and Saeki, a flying boat Chutai or Buntai (half-squadron) as well. Yokohama Kokutai was the first to be equipped solely with flying boats, initially with 12 H4H1s.

Production of the Type 97 built up slowly. During 1938, Kawanishi delivered eight Type 97 (H6K2) Model 11s before switching to building

The IJNAF accepted the 9-Shi Ogata Hiko Tei design as the Navy Type 97 Flying Boat Model 1 (H6K1). Kawanishi built four H6K1s which were assigned to Yokohama Kokutai in early 1938. Several of these early models were later modified into transport aircraft. Here, an early production H6K assigned to Yokohama Kokutai taxis up to a mooring buoy, probably near the unit's Yokohama base in 1938–39 (*AIR 40/2207, National Archives*) the Type 97 (H6K4) Model 22, which incorporated several improvements based on operational experience. Larger fuel tanks extended the range for reconnaissance missions to 3778 miles. As with many other Japanese aircraft of the period, H6K flying boats sacrificed protection for the fuel tanks for greater range. This would eventually prove to be the Type 97's Achilles' heel. During 1939 Kawanishi built 16 H6K4s, completing 20 during 1940. The company also developed the H6K2-L transport version of the Type 97 for the IJNAF.

A full Chutai had a nominal strength that often varied from the actual number of aircraft on hand. The full complement consisted of operational aircraft and a pool held in reserve and undergoing maintenance. Differences in nominal versus actual strength could be a function of production levels, organisation of new squadrons and a desire to conserve newly built aircraft by operating older models. In some cases, the Chutai at an IJNAF airfield might be assigned a Buntai instead of a full Chutai. A flying boat Chutai had a nominal complement of 14 aircraft and a Buntai had seven.

Unsurprisingly, the IJN was exceptionally secretive about the number of aircraft the IJNAF had on strength. In February 1938 the US Naval Attaché in Tokyo estimated that the IJNAF had 47 flying boats in service at five naval airfields around Japan, with four (Saeki, Sasebo, Tateyama and Yokohama) being considered operational units, with the Kokutai at Yokosuka focusing on training. A year later, the Royal Navy Attaché in Tokyo came up with a slightly different estimate, as follows;

Airfield	Flying Boat Type	Number of Squadrons	Operational Aircraft	Reserve Aircraft
Saeki	Type 91	½	4	2
Sasebo	Type 97	1	5	1
Tateyama	Type 90-2 and Type 91	½	3	0
		1	8	4
Yokohama	Type 97	1	5	1
Yokosuka	Type 15, Type 89 and Type 90-1	1	10 (training)	0

The IJNAF established one more dedicated flying boat unit before the start of the Pacific War. On 15 November 1940, Toko Kokutai became operational. The new air group was located at the port of the same name (now Donggang) on the southwestern coast of Formosa. Toko Kokutai received eight Type 97 flying boats transferred from Yokosuka Kokutai and began intensive training. Sasebo and Tateyama Kokutai each had a Chutai of flying boats but remained mixed air groups, operating reconnaissance seaplanes and other types as well as flying boats.

The flying boat units appear to have played a limited role in the initial years of the Second Sino-Japanese War. Soon after the start of the conflict in July 1937, the IJN blockaded all the major ports along the China coast prior to their eventual capture. Sea reconnaissance could be effectively done with floatplanes based on seaplane tenders, so there was less need for long-range flying boats. The IJNAF did employ small numbers of Type 91 flying boats, most likely from Sasebo Kokutai, for coastal patrols and as transports between China and the home islands.

In November 1939, Yokohama Kokutai was attached to the Fourth Fleet and assigned to patrol the islands in the Inner South Sea, principally the Bonin Islands. Once equipped with the Type 97, Yokohama Kokutai began flying patrols to the area around the Japanese Mandated Islands covering the Marianas, Marshall and Caroline Islands chains, operating from seaplane tenders. These training missions apparently included clandestine reconnaissance flights over the British Gilbert Islands.

The IJNAF also supported the effort of the Dai Nippon Kokutai K.K. (Japan Airways Company) to develop an air route to the South Pacific, arranging for the airline to acquire several H6K2s reconfigured as airliners, designated H6K2-Ls, with accommodation for passengers and freight. On 4 April 1939, an H6K2-L left Yokohama on the first flight to Palau, in the Carolines, via Saipan, returning to Yokohama six days later. The pilot on this first flight was Lt Cdr Nakagomi, who commanded one of the flying boat units in Yokohama Kokutai. In November 1940 his unit was assigned to the newly established Fourth Rengo Kokutai (Combined Air Group), under Combined Fleet control, and had its aircraft complement increased to 16 Type 97s. Its aircrews began training in torpedo attacks against shipping.

As the Type 97 entered production at the Kawanishi factory, the IJNAF was already looking forward to its replacement with an even more capable flying boat. The latest designs like the Short Sunderland, Sikorsky XPBS-1 and Boeing Model 314 featured all-metal construction, cantilever wings and more refined fuselage and flying surface elements with less drag. Hydrodynamic qualities improved with more refined V-bottom hulls, while greater aerodynamic efficiency from the lack of external bracing allowed higher maximum and cruising speeds. Air-cooled radial engines that produced increased power allowed greater maximum weights, meaning larger fuel loads for additional range and heavier armament. Flaps and controllable-pitch propellers allowed higher wing loadings for greater speed without the need for longer take-off or landing distances or fast landings. Flying boat manufacturers in America, Britain and Europe increasingly incorporated these advanced features in their designs.

To gain experience with this new generation of flying boats, the IJNAF purchased two Douglas DFs in December 1936. The American company had developed the all-metal, twin-engined, high-wing monoplane in the hope of selling it to Pan American Airways as a replacement for its older flying boats. Powered by two 1000 hp Wright Cyclone engines, the DF had a maximum speed of 178 mph, a cruising speed of 160 mph and a maximum range of 3300 miles when carrying 12 passengers.

The IJNAF purchased two Douglas DFs, giving one to Kawanishi to examine as an example of the new generation of all-metal flying boats coming into service in the late 1930s (*2008-3-31_image_553_01, Peter M Bowers Collection, MoF*)

The IJNAF's DF flying boats were ostensibly for Japan Airways, but were designated HXD-1 and HXD-2 for Navy Experimental Type D Flying Boat. The IJNAF gave one aircraft, HXD-1 (civilian registration J-ANET), to Kawanishi for evaluation. The second aircraft, HXD-2, with the civilian registration J-ANES, was lost at sea on 10 August 1938 when engine problems forced it to land in bad weather near the Bonin Islands while flying from Tokyo to Saipan.

Just 11 days after the loss of HXD-2, the IJNAF approached Kawanishi with a requirement to design a replacement for the Type 97 flying boat under the 13-Shi Ogata Hiko Tei (Large Flying Boat) Specification. Once again the IJNAF wanted Kawanishi to design a flying boat with superior performance to American or European aircraft then entering service. It required a maximum speed of 276 mph, a cruising speed of 184 mph and a cruising range on reconnaissance missions of 4603 miles – greater than any other large flying boat then in development. The IJNAF wanted what was for the time an impressive armament featuring five 20 mm cannon in turrets and four 7.7 mm machine guns, and the ability to carry 1995 kg of bombs or two 1000 kg torpedoes.

After a year of design effort and wind tunnel testing, Kawanishi began work on a prototype for the 13-Shi requirement in June 1939. Priority went to obtaining maximum cruising range. The design featured a shoulder-mounted wing with double-slotted flaps and four air-cooled radial engines in nacelles blended into the wing, a large vertical tail and fixed floats. Fortunately, Mitsubishi had developed the powerful Kasei 11 14-cylinder engine offering 1530 hp for take-off. Kawanishi chose four of these engines to power the design. The fuselage was deliberately kept narrower than the Type 97, but the height increased to accommodate the crew, equipment and fuel.

The prototype made its first flight on 29 December 1940 and, after testing and modifications, Kawanishi's new flying boat was officially accepted as the Navy Type 2 (H8K1) Flying Boat Model 11 (see *Osprey Duel 126 – H6K "Type 97"/H8K "Emily" vs PB4Y-1/2 Liberator/Privateer* for more details on development of the H8K). During 1941, Kawanishi completed only three more H8K1 prototypes. As a result, the IJNAF's two flying boat units, Toko and Yokohama Kokutai, went to war with the Type 97 (H6K4).

The Kawanishi 13-Shi Ogata Hiko Tei prototype takes off from Kobe Harbour, near the company's factory in Osaka, during testing in early 1941. To resolve spray problems encountered during early take-off runs, Kawanishi deepened the hull of the 13-Shi prototype and added longitudinal strips between the keel and the main chine, seen in this photograph, to divert the water (*2008-3-31_image_511_01, Peter M Bowers Collection, MoF*)

On 15 January 1941, the IJNAF introduced a new organisational system for its units. Eleventh Koku Kantai (Air Fleet) was formed, consisting of 21st, 22nd and 23rd Koku Sentai (Air Flotillas) comprised of eight land-based Kokutai. The establishment of Eleventh Koku Kantai enabled the Koku Sentai to come under a single operational command for better coordination in time of war, which seemed increasingly likely. That same day Toko Kokutai was assigned to 21st Koku Sentai. The Kokutai received an additional eight H6K4s and began undertaking patrols over the South China Sea out to a distance of 700 miles from base.

Separately, Fourth Rengo Kokutai was redesignated 24th Koku Sentai and, with Yokohama Kokutai and Chitose Kokutai (flying Type 96 G3M land-based attack bombers) as its component units, was assigned to the Fourth Fleet which was responsible for covering the Mandated Islands in the Central Pacific.

In February 1941 Yokohama Kokutai's 12 Type 97 flying boats flew to Saipan for several months of training in long-range reconnaissance, bombing and air-to-air gunnery. Over the summer the Kokutai flew regularly between Saipan and the Marshall Islands, becoming familiar with the area where it would go to war. In the weeks before the start of the fighting in the Pacific, the two flying boat Kokutai moved to their wartime stations. Each had by now received a full complement of 24 Type 97 flying boats.

Toko Kokutai advanced to Palau on 8 November 1941, taking 18 Type 97 H6K4 flying boats and two H6K2-L transports, and leaving six H6K4s as a reserve. On 26 November Yokohama Kokutai left Japan for Saipan, arriving at Imieji, a small island in the Jaluit Atoll in the Marshall Islands where the IJNAF maintained a seaplane base, with eight Type 97 H6K4 flying boats and three H6K2-L transports 48 hours later. Yokohama Kokutai also sent 16 Type 97 H6K4s and five H6K2-Ls to Maloelap, east of Jaluit, where the IJNAF had another seaplane base.

Sasebo Kokutai remained in Japan with 16 carrier-based fighters, six reconnaissance seaplanes and 15 H6K4s, which it used to patrol the home islands. Sometime during 1941, Tateyama Kokutai gave up its small flying boat unit. It may never have operated the H6K flying boat at all.

By the start of the Pacific War, the IJNAF had nearly two decades of experience in maritime patrol aviation. From modest beginnings the IJN had built up a flying boat component within its naval air arm that could traverse the Pacific in world class aircraft with exceptional range.

There were, however, limitations to the IJNAF's maritime patrol aviation that would hinder the flying boat units during the Pacific War. Kawanishi never had the production capacity of comparable American manufacturers. Between 1939–45, the company built 382 Type 97 H6K and Type 2 H8K flying boats. In contrast, between 1940–45 Consolidated constructed 2182 PBY Catalina flying boats. This meant that as the war intensified, Kawanishi would be hard pressed to make good combat and operational losses in the flying boat units.

Furthermore, as historian Mark Peattie pointed out, in a Navy obsessed with the offensive, reconnaissance crews did not always receive adequate training, while their limited numbers put a great strain on the crews as they flew mission after mission without relief.

CHAPTER TWO

FLYING BOAT KOKUTAI DECEMBER 1941–APRIL 1942

An H6K4 takes off somewhere in the Pacific. In the early months of the war, the flying boats retained their pre-war overall grey scheme. Note how the Japanese censor has removed any unit markings from the tail of this aircraft (*ShinMaywa Industries, Ltd*)

The IJNAF would go to war with just two flying boat units to cover the vast expanse of the Pacific. Japan's objective was to capture vital raw materials in Southeast Asia critical to its economic survival, particularly petroleum from the Netherlands East Indies (NEI – now Indonesia).

The opening phase of the Japanese war plan covered the capture of Southeast Asia in three stages. First, capturing American positions at Guam, Wake Island and the British Gilbert Islands to set up a defensive barrier on Japan's eastern flank, while in the west, occupying Thailand, northern Malaya, British Borneo and commencing the invasion of the Philippines. Second, completing the capture of Malaya, invading Burma, capturing the northern islands in the NEI and seizing the Bismarck Archipelago to extend the eastern defensive barrier. Third, completing the capture of the NEI and Burma. The Japanese defensive barrier would then extend from the Andaman Islands in the Indian Ocean, through the NEI to New Guinea and the Bismarck Islands, and north from the Gilbert Islands to the Kuriles in northern Japan.

The IJNAF's two flying boat units were heavily involved in the advance, but since they were assigned to different fleets in different areas, their operations will be covered separately.

TOKO KOKUTAI

21st Koku Sentai was assigned to the Southern Task Force. Its mission was to attack American shipping off the coast of the Philippines and escort Japanese invasion forces as they moved south towards the NEI, covering the eastern approaches to the Dutch colony. The IJN had responsibility for supporting Imperial Japanese Army (IJA) troops in areas south of the Philippines. The Japanese plan was to advance under an air umbrella, gaining control of the skies before pushing air cover forward towards the next objective, repeating the process again and again.

During the first few months of the war Toko Kokutai would provide regular reconnaissance ahead of the advance towards the NEI, moving south from base to base through the Celebes and attacking shipping and land targets as the opportunity arose. In the days leading up to the start of the war Toko Kokutai flew regular patrol missions out of Palau, with up to 14 flying boats undertaking reconnaissance flights.

Elements of the IJA's 16th Army had assembled at Palau for landings at Legaspi, on southern Luzon, at Davao, on the southeast coast of Mindanao, and on Jolo, the capital of the Sulu Archipelago southwest of the main Philippine Islands. Transports carrying the Legaspi landing force left Palau on the morning of 7 December with an accompanying naval escort that included the carrier *Ryujo*.

The following day (still 7 December 1941 east of the International Date Line), Toko Kokutai sent out four Type 97s to patrol sectors from 239 to 320 degrees from Palau – effectively the seas north and south of Mindanao – covering the intended route of the Legaspi landing force. The 16th Army came ashore at Legaspi on 12 December.

The forces for the landings at Davao and Jolo left Palau on 17 December. In the days leading up to the force's departure and advance to Davao, Toko Kokutai flew patrols towards Mindanao and beyond, covering the seas around the islands and to the south, carrying out several attacks on *Marine Luchtvaart Dienst* (MLD–Dutch Naval Air Service) seaplane bases. The day after the Davao Landing Force's departure the Kokutai sent out 22 flying boats to patrol around Davao and north to Cebu. Some of the missions were as long as 13 hours in duration.

Toko Kokutai flew its first bombing mission of the war on 15 December when three H6K4s dropped fifteen 60 kg bombs on Cebu. The next day, a single H6K4 attacked the MLD seaplane base at Sorong, in Netherlands New Guinea, at 1030 hrs, aiming for but missing the Dutch seaplane tender *Arend*. Two MLD Dornier Do 24 flying boats tried to intercept the H6K4, but they could not catch it. Around this date the seaplane tender USS *Langley* (AV-3) stopped at Menado, at the tip of the Celebes, to refuel US Navy PBY Catalinas. A single H6K4 on patrol came in and dropped several bombs on the vessel, but they all missed. Two H6K4s also reported an attack on three American submarines south-southeast of Davao, claiming them sunk.

A single H6K4 returned to Sorong on 17 December, dropping out of the clouds to bomb an MLD Do 24 on the water. Again, the crew missed its target. That same day, another H6K4 attacked the now-abandoned MLD seaplane base at Ternate, off Halmahera Island, dropping bombs on a Dutch patrol vessel that escaped unscathed. On this occasion,

Toko Kokutai joined G4M1 ('Betty') bombers of Kanoya Kokutai in an attack on Cebu on 22 December 1941. The H6K4s often accompanied both the G3M and G4M Land-based Attack Bombers on their missions against Allied bases and shipping during the first phase of the Japanese war plan in Southeast Asia in 1941–42 (*Author's Collection*)

MLD Do 24 X-30 appeared on the scene as the Type 97 was departing. After a 25-minute chase, the Dornier caught up with the H6K4 and opened fire in what was likely the first aerial combat between rival flying boats in the Pacific War. The Dutch tail gunner damaged the H6K4's starboard inboard engine and shredded an aileron, but his IJNAF counterpart knocked out the Dornier's middle engine with his 20 mm cannon, forcing it to break off the combat.

Remarkably, another aerial combat occurred three days later when a pair of MLD Do 24s encountered two patrolling H6K4s. The flying boats exchanged fire and one of the Dorniers, X-22, was damaged and had to return to base.

The 16th Army captured Davao and its airfield on 20 December, and two days later Toko Kokutai commenced shifting its base there when an advance force of nine H6K4s departed Palau. By 25 December – the date of the landings on Jolo – 19 flying boats of the Kokutai had shifted to Davao, while four went temporarily to Legaspi.

Toko Kokutai continued flying operations without interruption while transferring to Davao. On 21 December eight H6K4s and six Type 0 (F1M 'Pete') Observation Seaplanes bombed the airfield at Del Monte, on Mindanao's northern coast. The next day, several Toko Kokutai flying boats joined Type 1 (G4M 'Betty') Land-based Attack Bombers from Kanoya Kokutai in a raid on Cebu, where the formations claimed one 5000-ton ship sunk. From Davao, Toko Kokutai sent its patrols to the south, covering Menado at the northeast tip of the Celebes and the seas around the islands, in search of Allied shipping.

The MLD struck back against Toko Kokutai on 23 December when a small force of six Do 24s targeted Davao, attacking nine H6K4s on the water and bombing the waterfront dock area and shipping in the harbour. The Dutch pilots thought they had set several of the Japanese flying boats on fire, but none were lost. Toko Kokutai did suffer its first casualties the next day, however, when a US Army Air Corps (USAAC) P-40E on a reconnaissance mission over Davao spotted three H6K4s on the water. Although ordered not to attack, 1Lt John Brownewell of the 17th Pursuit Squadron (PS) could not resist the temptation, dropping down from

10,000 ft and making three passes over the flying boats. Although one of the H6K4s got off, a second flying boat was set on fire and ran aground, where it soon blew up.

Toko Kokutai experienced its second combat loss on the last day of the year. During the final week of December, it had flown reconnaissance missions every day, sending out three to six flying boats south to cover the Celebes, Halmahera, Borneo and the seas in between. On one of these reconnaissance missions on 28 December, four H6K4s encountered the destroyer USS *Peary* (DD-226) en route to Java. One of the flying boats dropped six 60 kg bombs and another apparently strafed the vessel with 20 mm and 7.7 mm guns.

On 30 December eight H6K4s bombed Cebu, claiming to have sunk a merchant ship. The next day, two sections of Toko Kokutai flying boats attacked the seaplane tender USS *Heron* (AVP-2) as the ship was returning to its base in Ambon from delivering oil and parts to a damaged destroyer off Halmahera. After hiding from one air attack in a rain squall, *Heron* emerged to see an H6K4 on the surface off to starboard. The flying boat quickly took off and circled over the vessel for nearly four hours.

In the early afternoon *Heron*'s crew spotted two sections of six H6K4s approaching. The first section of three aircraft made three bombing runs on the ship, but each time *Heron* evaded the bombs. The second section of aircraft then came in to bomb the seaplane tender, but on the first run one of *Heron*'s two three-inch guns hit one of the attacking flying boats, which flew off to the north trailing smoke. Although *Heron* again evaded the bombs, five twin-engined bombers and three more flying boats soon joined the attack on the small ship.

The twin-engined bombers dropped several bombs, one of which struck the ship's mainmast and three more hit near the port bow, damaging one of the vessel's two three-inch guns, killing a sailor and wounding several more. The three flying boats then made a torpedo attack, coming in from the port and starboard sides. When *Heron* defeated the torpedoes by deft manoeuvring, the flying boats came back to strafe the ship, wounding more of the crew and inflicting further damage. The solitary undamaged three-inch gun hit the flying boat of Lt Juso Ota, forcing him to ditch. *Heron*'s fire also damaged the remaining two flying boats, forcing their crews (who, somewhat optimistically, reported that they had attacked a 'cruiser') to beach the aircraft on their return to Davao. Although half of *Heron*'s crew were wounded, the survivors brought the damaged ship back to Ambon.

The poor condition of captured airfields in the Philippines delayed the start

The gallant ship USS *Heron* (AVP-2), formerly a Lapwing-class minesweeper that had been converted into a seaplane carrier, fought off attacks from six Toko Kokutai H6K4s and land-based attack bombers on 31 December 1941 as the vessel headed for its base at Ambon. Fire from *Heron*'s solitary operable three-inch gun hit Lt Juso Ota's H6K4, forcing him to ditch. Two other flying boats were also damaged (*Naval History and Heritage Command (NHHC)*)

of the second stage of the Southern Expedition, but on 2 January 1942 the order came to commence operations. The aviation elements of the offensive were organised into Air Raid Units, combining air and landing forces. The 1st Air Raid Unit consisted of 21st Koku Sentai, with a detachment of Kanoya Kokutai with Type 1 (G4M) land-based attack bombers, 1st Kokutai with Type 96 (G3M) land-based attack bombers, 3rd Kokutai with Type 0 (A6M) fighters, Toko Kokutai and the IJN's Yokohama Special Naval Landing Force (SNLF).

The objective of the air units was to support the advance of the Eastern Attack Unit to capture Menado at the northern tip of the Celebes, then, successively, Kendari at the centre of the Celebes, Makassar at the southern end of the the island of Ambon, Kupang on the island of Timor and, finally, Bali, thus securing the eastern flank of the assault on the NEI.

On the night of 6 January 1942, Toko Kokutai planned an audacious attack on Ambon with six H6K4s together with 21 G4M bombers from Kanoya Kokutai. Cdr Tatsuo Aizawa led one of the flying boat sections. His and another aircraft were armed with two torpedoes each, while the third flying boat carried flares only for illumination. The attack called for the third flying boat to fly over the harbour at Ambon dropping flares, while Aizawa and the second flying boat landed on the water and released their torpedoes at moored ships before taking off again.

Whether such an attack method would have worked became moot when Aizawa's H6K4 developed engine trouble on take-off, hit the mast of a cargo ship in Davao harbour and crashed, killing the entire crew. The torpedo attack was called off, but the two flying boats and the second section of H6K4s continued with the mission, joining the Kanoya bombers in hitting the airfield at Ambon.

The Toko H6K4s returned to Ambon the next day for a raid on the airfield at Laha. Taking off from Davao, two flying boats arrived over the target at 0345 hrs, and according to some sources several more attacked nearby Halong airfield – it may be that only two flying boats attacked both airfields, as the mission report lists just the two aircraft on the Laha mission. The flying boats made four separate attacks on the airfield, expending 24 60 kg bombs, then dropped down to strafe the airfields, damaging several buildings, two Royal Australian Air Force (RAAF) Hudson bombers from No 13 Sqn and a Netherlands East Indies Army B-339 Buffalo fighter. One of the Hudson pilots tried to get revenge three days later when he encountered an H6K4 while escorting an American PBY Catalina. The Hudson gunners fired on the H6K4 but apparently did little damage.

Japanese forces captured the town of Menado on 11 January 1942, with Yokohama SNLF paratroopers being used for the first time. In the days leading up to the landings, Toko Kokutai flew patrols over the Celebes and the Molucca Seas searching for Allied warships, with land-based attack bombers standing by to engage them, but none were found. On the day of the landings, two flying boats (one of which was an H6K2-L transport) alighted on Lake Tondano, south of Menado, with 22 soldiers on board from the Yokohama SNLF – a medical team, an anti-tank unit and the paymaster.

During the attack on the 11th, Japanese forces also captured the town of Kema on the coast opposite Menado. The IJNAF subsequently moved units to the airfield near Kema, first fighters and then land attack bombers. Eight Toko Kokutai flying boats also arrived on 17 January, followed by a further 14 the next day. The unit apparently shifted to Kema shortly thereafter, where it remained until mid-February, sending detachments to forward bases as necessary. The Kokutai commenced patrolling just 24 hours after arriving at its new home.

After a land-based reconnaissance aeroplane reported enemy submarines in the Molucca Sea east of the Celebes, Toko Kokutai had been ordered to patrol the area in search of such vessels. Its crews flew 41 search missions but found only whales. The search was called off on 19 January and the Kokuti went back to long-range patrols covering the seas to the south and east of the Celebes, searching for enemy shipping, carrying out reconnaissance of the area around Ambon and attacking Laha airfield again. On 21 January an H6K4 undertook a reconnaissance flight over the airfield with an escort of Zero-sen fighters. Later that day two flying boats returned to strafe anti-aircraft positions around Laha airfield, before Zero-sens came in to strafe. The flying boats returned to attack the airfield on 22, 23 and 24 January.

On one patrol mission covering the Banda Sea near Ambon on 23 January, an H6K4 had a run in with a No 13 Sqn Hudson escorting a transport ship. Sighting the approaching aircraft flown by Flt Lt Les Ingram, the H6K4 dived down to 100 ft above the sea. Ingram jettisoned his bombs to gain more speed and made four attacks on the H6K4 from the starboard and port quarters and one from astern. He used up all the ammunition in his front guns, and later reported that he had hit the H6K4 in the fuselage.

The Japanese were unaware that RAAF Hudsons and US Navy PBYs had been using an airfield at Namlea on the nearby island of Buru until a patrolling Type 97 happened to see a Hudson emerge from the clouds below on 24 January – the two aeroplanes almost colliding. Curious, the flying boat descended below the cloud layer to discover the base, dropping four bombs which did little damage. The next day another flying boat returned to Namlea, followed 30 minutes later by 16 land-based attack bombers that targeted the airfield but did little damage. Nevertheless, both Namlea and Laha were evacuated shortly thereafter as the southern advance continued. Japanese forces seized Kendari on 24 January, landed on the island of Ambon one week later and captured Makassar on 9 February.

On 1 February, Toko Kokutai sent a detachment of four flying boats to operate from Kendari for ten days, leaving 17 aircraft at Kema, apparently operating from nearby Lake Tondano. The mission now was to search for enemy shipping to the south in the Banda Sea.

The third stage of the advance, seizing the NEI, began in early February with attacks to eliminate Allied air power over Java prior to an invasion. On the 3rd, fighters based at Balikpapan and land-based attack bombers flying from Kendari targeted eastern Java. Toko Kokutai set up a rescue unit to support the air offensive, sending one flying boat to the island of Laoet, off the southeast tip of Borneo, and to Kangean Island, northeast of eastern Java.

Late on the night of 3 February two Toko Kokutai flying boats, delayed by bad weather, took off to search for enemy shipping sighted earlier in the day. This was a combined force of American and Dutch cruisers and destroyers seeking a Japanese convoy coming down the Makassar Strait. One of the H6K4s spotted three cruisers and two destroyers at around 0400 hrs on 4 February and shadowed the Allied ships until 0600 hrs, when the aircraft headed back to Kendari. The second flying boat found one cruiser with four destroyers at 0537 hrs, shadowing this group until it too had to head back to Kendari at 0630 hrs.

Later that morning a force of 60 Type 1 G4M bombers from Kanoya, Takao and 1st Kokutai on a mission to bomb Surabaya, in eastern Java, were diverted to attack the Allied ships, hitting the Dutch cruiser HNLMS *De Ruyter* and the American cruisers USS *Houston* (CA-30) and USS *Marblehead* (CL-12). Lacking fighter protection the Allied vessels had little choice but to withdraw. Failing to locate the retreating ships later that night, Toko Kokutai returned to regular patrolling and convoy escort.

Even before Japanese forces completed the capture of Ambon on 3 February, Toko Kokutai sent four flying boats to begin operating from the island, with 12 more arriving on 7 February and a further six three days later. With the full Kokutai now at Ambon, it commenced patrolling further to the south into the Timor Sea and beyond in search of Allied shipping. These patrols were uneventful until 15 February, when three H6K4s flying over the Arafura Sea, east of Timor, sighted a convoy of seven ships, with *Houston* as escort, heading towards Timor. The flying boats followed the convoy for three hours and dropped several 60 kg bombs before heading back to base as their fuel ran low.

The convoy had radioed Darwin that it was being shadowed by Japanese flying boats, and in response the RAAF base commander despatched a USAAC P-40E from the 21st PS. 2Lt Robert Buel found the flying boats and attacked the H6K4 flown by Sub Lt Mirau. New to combat, Buel made the mistake of attacking the flying boat from the rear. Rounds from the 20 mm tail gun hit his P-40, killing Buel and sending his fighter crashing into the sea. However, prior to his demise, Buel had set the H6K4 on fire and killed Mirau. The flying boat also crashed into the sea, with five crew surviving both the impact and 11 days in a raft before reaching the Australian coast, where they were captured.

The following day (16th), nine H6K4s took off from Ambon to lead 36 G3M bombers from 1st Kokutai in an attack on the convoy. The flying boats dropped nine 250 kg and twenty-seven 60 kg bombs, scoring several near misses that apparently damaged but failed to sink any of the ships. The G3Ms damaged two of the transports in the convoy badly enough to force the vessels to return to Darwin, where they would be sunk in strikes by carrier-based IJNAF aircraft on 19 February.

From then until early March, Toko Kokutai patrolled over the Timor and Arafura Seas searching for Allied shipping withdrawing from Java following the Japanese landings on 28 February. With the capture of Timor three days earlier, Toko Kokutai transferred 12 H6K4s from Ambon to Semau, a small island near Koepang (now Kupang) on the southern tip of the island. From here, the flying boats ranged 690 miles to the southwest of Timor.

Prior to the transfer, on 20 February, off the Kimberley coast of Western Australia, a Toko Kokutai H6K4 spotted the merchant vessel

MV *Koolama* at 1130 hrs bound for Darwin and attacked it, doing no damage. Two hours later, three more H6K4s, led by Lt Cdr Tsunaki Yonehara, attacked the ship, dropping 24 60 kg bombs that disabled the 4000-ton vessel and forced it to beach in nearby Rulhieres Bay. Although MV *Koolama* was subsequently refloated and sailed to Wyndham, it sunk in shallow waters there on 3 March.

20 February also saw another Toko Kokutai H6K4 in action after its crew sighted the corvette HMAS *Warrnambool* rescuing survivors from the transport vessel *Don Isidro*, which had been sunk by IJNAF carrier aircraft off Melville Island during the previous day's Darwin attack. The flying boat targeted the Australian warship (which had survived the Darwin raid unscathed), but its crew used a smoke screen and sharp manoeuvring to avoid being hit.

On 2 and 3 March Toko Kokutai H6K4s undertook reconnaissance flights over the town of Broome, on the Kimberley coast of Western Australia, in preparation for a damaging raid on the latter date by Zero-sen fighters of 3rd Kokutai from Koepang. The H6K4s again went out on patrol on the 4th, and at least one made a post-attack reconnaissance flight over Broome, while another strafed a Koninklijke Nederlandsch-Indische Luchtvaart Maatschappij DC-3 that Zero-sens from the Broome raid had shot up and forced down on a beach 50 miles north of the town. The patrols out of Koepang continued into the middle of March, when Toko Kokutai was transferred west to support Japanese advances in the Indian Ocean.

The Southern Operation intended to capture Malaya, northern Sumatra, in the NEI, and all of Burma. To protect its western flank against possible attacks across the Indian Ocean, the IJN's Combined Fleet decided to strike the Royal Navy's Eastern Fleet and its bases in Ceylon (now Sri Lanka) and shipping in the Bay of Bengal. The IJN determined that it was important to capture the Andaman Islands, approximately 400 miles from Rangoon, to defend Burma, Malaya and northern Sumatra. After the fall of Java on 9 March, Toko Kokutai sent seven H6K4s to Penang, on the west coast of Malaya, in preparation for moving to Port Blair on the Andaman Islands. The flying boats arrived at Penang on 13 March, having flown via Kendari and Singapore.

The outnumbered British garrison at Port Blair surrendered to the Japanese on 23 March, and the following day all seven H6K4s flew in from Penang. The main body of Toko Kokutai also moved, heading to Batavia (now Jakarta), on Java, to support the detachment at Port Blair.

The 4000-ton MV *Koolama* rolled on its side whilst in the port of Wyndham on 3 March 1942, having been badly damaged by twenty-four 60 kg bombs dropped from four Toko Kokutai H6K4s on 20 February. The Darwin-bound vessel, owned by the Western Australian Shipping Service, survived the attack thanks to excellent seamanship by its crew. The hull was eventually raised in 1948, after which it was towed out to sea and scuttled (*Peter Ingman Collection*)

On 25 March the flying boats began performing reconnaissance patrols out to a distance of some 690 miles southwest of Port Blair towards Ceylon. The IJNAF had established three patrol sectors – C, D and E – covering the Bay of Bengal from Ceylon up to Calcutta. Three flying boats went out daily to cover one of the sectors, with instructions not to fly closer than 150 miles from the Indian coast. The H6K4 crews saw nothing on their patrols on 26 and 27 March, but on the 28th, while patrolling Sector E closest to Calcutta, a pair of flying boats sighted two merchant ships and attacked, stopping one in the water with a near miss. On 29 March the patrolling flying boats searching Sector C nearest to Ceylon attacked another merchant ship, claiming to have scored one hit.

As the Combined Fleet neared Ceylon for its strike on the Eastern Fleet, Toko Kokutai began pushing its patrols out to 805 miles from Port Blair, flying close enough to Ceylon on 1 April to report on aircraft spotted at RAF China Bay, near the Royal Naval Dockyard, Trincomalee, and to count ships in Trincomalee Bay.

The following day, three H6K4s searched Sector D, attacking two large merchant ships and claiming damage to both with near misses. SS *Orestes* reported being attacked by three flying boats, but its crew kept them away with anti-aircraft fire. On 3 April three H6K4s patrolled Sector E, at the northern end of the Bay of Bengal, spotting 13 merchant ships in the Ganges Delta near Calcutta. The flying boats attacked a large merchant ship estimated at 28,000 tons, and two smaller vessels, with each H6K4 dropping two 250 kg bombs. The crews involved claimed to have sunk the large merchantman and damaged the remaining two vessels, but none of the ships were hit in the attack.

On 4 April, 24 hours before the Combined Fleet's Easter Sunday Raid on the Ceylonese capital Colombo, Toko Kokutai sent out a lone H6K4 to reconnoitre military targets in Trincomalee and three more flying boats to search the Bay of Bengal for any Royal Navy warships. The unit continued mounting daily patrols during the Combined Fleet's strike on Colombo on 5 April and Trincomalee four days later, its aircraft also attacking Allied shipping in the Bay of Bengal.

The RAF had received reports that the IJNAF was using Port Blair as a base for flying boat operations, and on 11 April a Hudson crew from No 139 Sqn confirmed this when it spotted nine H6K4s there. Two Hudsons from the unit targeted Port Blair just before dawn on the 14th, sinking one H6K4 and damaging 12 more. Two more Hudsons made a follow-up attack shortly after dawn, sinking two more H6K4s and shooting up eight. A solitary IJNAF Zero-sen attacked the fleeing RAF bombers as they headed for Akyab, in Burma, and shot one down.

With other aircraft nearly worn out from constant use, these attacks were damaging. Indeed, for the rest of April and well into May Toko Kokutai could only send out one or two flying boats on patrol from Port Blair until more reinforcements arrived from Japan. One exception was an attack on Akyab on 30 April, when five H6K4s dropped fifty-eight 60 kg bombs.

Following the Combined Fleet's withdrawal from the Indian Ocean, Toko Kokutai maintained a detachment at Port Blair until August 1942, when an urgent need for reinforcements would see it move to Rabaul to support operations in the Solomon Islands.

YOKOHAMA KOKUTAI

For Yokohama Kokutai, the Pacific War began on 8 December 1941 with a massed formation flight of 15 H6K4s, which must have been a sight to behold, from their temporary base at Majuro Atoll, in the Marshall Islands, where they had moved on 6 December in preparation for the mission to bomb Howland Island, 950 miles distant. Part way to their target, bad weather forced the formation to return to Majuro. Yokohama Kokutai also sent out two flying boats from Imieji to bomb radio stations on Narau and Ocean Islands, dropping six 60 kg bombs that did little damage.

A formation of H6K4s on patrol. One of the flying boats remains in the pre-war scheme of light grey overall. Fifteen flying boats flying in close formation would have been quite a sight – Yokohama Kokutai attempted such a massed formation flight when it tried to bomb Howland Island on 8 December 1941. Weather defeated the unit on this occasion, however (*80G-169790, RG80, NARA*)

The day after the start of the war, Yokohama Kokutai flew a return mission to Howland Island with 15 H6K4s, and this time the flying boats dropped twenty 250 kg and one hundred and twenty 60 kg bombs and expended 72 rounds of 20 mm and 337 rounds of 7.7 mm ammunition.

Yokohama Kokutai also sent three flying boats back to Narau and Ocean Islands on 9 December, where they dropped four 250 kg and twenty-four 60 kg bombs and strafed with their 20 mm tail turret guns and 7.7 mm machine guns. A great deal of damage was done to the radio station on Ocean Island. On 11 December four flying boats returned to Narau, dropping two 250 kg bombs and forty-two 60 kg bombs.

Shortly thereafter, the Fourth Fleet ordered Yokohama Kokutai to support the invasion of Wake Island, rather than continue its offensive against Narau and Ocean Islands.

Yokohama Kokutai's first attack on Wake took place on the night of 11 December when five H6K4s left Majuro at 1900 hrs. Three flying boats had to return before reaching Wake, leaving the formation leader, Lt Cdr Soichi Tashiro and Special Duty Ensign Unekichi Nakano to continue on. They arrived over the target at around 0530 hrs on 12 December, each flying boat dropping four 250 kg and twelve 60 kg bombs around the island. Capts Herbert Freuler and Frank Tharin from VMF-211 had taken off in their Wildcats to intercept the flying boats, and the latter chased Nakano's H6K4 and shot it down. It was the first Type 97 flying boat to be lost in World War 2.

Yokohama Kokutai sent out 11 H6K4s on the night of 13 December, with ten arriving over Wake at around 0340 hrs on the 14th. They dropped a mix of 250 kg and 60 kg bombs, apparently without doing any damage. Yokohama Kokutai flying boats went out on a mission to Wake again the next day, with crews completing nearly 12 hours of flying time. Eight flying boats took off but one aborted. The remaining seven dropped ten 250 kg and sixty 60 kg bombs on the northern part of the island, after which they strafed the area near some of the US Marine Corps gun batteries, expending 337 rounds of 20 mm and 1429 rounds of 7.7 mm ammunition with little effect.

After the Japanese seized Makin Island in the Gilbert Islands group, Yokohama Kokutai sent three H6K4s to the former and tasked crews with undertaking long-range reconnaissance patrols, while still contributing to the attacks on Wake. The next such strike took place on 17 December (16 December at Pearl Harbor) when Lt Cdr Tashiro again led eight H6K4s to Wake, arriving over Peale Island 30 minutes after sunset. The flying boats targeted the gun batteries on Peale, strafing them with 378 rounds of 20 mm and 117 rounds of 7.7 mm ammunition. Again, no damage was done.

This proved to be the last attack made by Yokohama Kokutai on Wake. For the rest of December it flew patrols to the east of the island and around the Gilbert Islands from bases at Makin Island, Wotje and Imieji, in the Marshall Islands, and Wake Island after its capture on 23 December.

On 17 December Yokohama Kokutai received orders to transfer three flying boats from Makin to the IJN base at Truk, before heading on to Christmas Island (also known as Kapingamarangi Island) to undertake reconnaissance missions of New Britain in preparation for the next stage of the advance. By early January 1942, Yokohama Kokutai had 14 flying boats at Truk, three at Wake Island, four at Imieji (Jaluit Atoll) and three at Makin Island.

The first stage of Japanese operations in the Central Pacific sought to capture Guam, Wake Island and the Gilbert Islands. Once this had been achieved, the second stage of operations commenced with the aim being to capture the islands in the Bismarck Archipelago. They would provide a barrier against attacks on the base at Truk, as well as giving access to the Coral Sea and New Guinea to the southwest. The key objective was Rabaul, in New Britain, which possessed an excellent natural harbour. The RAAF had also established airfields there at Lakunai and Vunakanau, as well as facilities for flying boats. At 650 miles from Truk, Rabaul was well within the range of IJNAF flying boats and land-based attack bombers.

After transferring flying boats to Truk and Greenwich Island, Yokohama Kokutai flew its first reconnaissance of the Bismarcks on 20 December, sending one H6K4 from Truk to Kavieng, on New Ireland, and a second aircraft from Greenwich Island to Rabaul. Single flying boats returned to Rabaul on 21 and 25 December. The RAAF had several Wirraway light bomber/ground attack aircraft at Rabaul, but they did not have the performance to catch the IJNAF flying boats.

On 3 January 1942, the commander of the South Seas Detachment, charged with the capture of Rabaul, ordered Chitose Kokutai (also based at Truk with G3M land-based attack bombers) and Yokohama Kokutai to initiate attacks on the town, beginning the next day, in preparation for the invasion scheduled for later in the month. Chitose Kokutai G3Ms made the first attack on 4 January, targeting Lakunai airfield, while Yokohama Kokutai sent eight H6K4s to Rabaul just as dusk was falling. The flying boats dropped ten 250 kg and eighty 60 kg bombs but failed to hit their target. They all returned to Truk shortly after midnight.

Nine H6K4s targeted Rabaul two days later, bombing Vunakanau airfield from 12,000 ft. On this occasion, for once, the bombing was successful, with fourteen 250 kg and sixty-six 60 kg bombs destroying a newly built direction-finding station and control hut and a Wirraway, and damaging a Hudson. The attack also left the runway temporarily unserviceable. Four Wirraways from No 24 Sqn had hurriedly taken off to intercept the flying boats, and one, flown by Flt Lt B H Anderson, got to within 300 yards of one of the IJNAF aircraft. Although the pilot expended all of his ammunition (the Wirraway had two fixed 0.303-in Vickers Mk V machine guns mounted directly ahead of the cockpit), he failed to inflict any damage. The H6K4s, in turn, fired off several hundred 20 mm and 7.7 mm rounds at the Wirraway, again without effect.

With the capture of Rabaul on 23 January, the South Seas Force commander ordered Yokohama Kokutai to advance there from Truk. However, due to RAAF attacks on the town, the Kokutai moved eight H6K4s temporarily to Green Island, east of New Ireland, which the Japanese had seized that same day. This detachment returned to Rabaul on 4 February, as did three flying boats that had remained at Truk. Yokohama Kokutai now had responsibility for patrolling southeast from Rabaul along the Solomon Islands chain out to a distance of 700 miles, and for conducting reconnaissance over New Guinea.

Prior to transferring to Rabaul, Yokohama Kokutai flew two reconnaissance missions to Port Moresby, in New Guinea, on 22 and 23 January. It followed these up on 28 and 29 January, when flying boats returned to Port Moresby from Rabaul. Having reconnoitred Salamaua and Wau, in New Guinea, on 31 January, nine H6K4s returned to the latter the following day to bomb and strafe the town's airfield, causing damage to buildings and wounding several civilians.

While the main unit of Yokohama Kokutai moved from Truk to Rabaul, it had retained detachments of six flying boats (of which three were serviceable) at Imieji and three at Makin for patrols over the Central Pacific, covering specific sectors to the east. These detachments had the misfortune of running into the first US Navy carrier strikes of the war, and what would prove to be the nemesis of the IJNAF's flying boat units – carrier-borne fighter aircraft.

On 1 February, Adm William Halsey's Task Force (TF) 8, which included the aircraft carrier USS *Enterprise* (CV-6), launched attacks against Wotje, Kwajalein and Maloelap, while Adm Frank Jack Fletcher's TF 17, including the aircraft carrier USS *Yorktown* (CV-5), went after Jaluit and Mili, in the Marshall Islands, and Makin Island in the Gilberts.

Just after 0400 hrs, nine SBD-3 Dauntless dive-bombers of VS-5 arrived over Makin to find two H6K4s moored below. The SBDs dropped down to strafe the flying boats. In their first attack they hit a fuel tank and bombs on board one of the flying boats, blowing it up. As the crew of the second H6K4 hastily prepared to take off in an attempt to escape, the SBDs returned for a second strafing run and again struck the flying boat in the fuel tank causing it to explode. All five crew perished.

Lt(jg) E Scott McCuskey, sitting in the cockpit of an F4F-4 Wildcat, with Ens George Gay, the sole survivor of VT-8, after the Battle of Midway. As a member of VF-42, McCuskey was the first US Navy carrier fighter pilot to shoot down a Japanese flying boat in World War 2 – he and Ens John Adams combined to destroy an H6K4 on 1 February off the Gilbert Islands (*NH-90482, NHHC*)

None of the flying boats at Imieji were hit in the attack, and shortly after the US Navy aircraft had departed, all three serviceable H6K4s took off to search for the American task force. One of the flying boats, dodging in and out of cloud, reached a position ten miles from *Yorktown*, whereupon two F4F Wildcats from VF-42, flown by Ens E Scott McCuskey and Ens John Adams, intercepted the flying boat, knocking out its tail turret in their first pass. In their second pass, McCuskey came in from below, firing at the keel and wings, while Adams attacked from behind the Type 97, which burst into flames and exploded, blowing off the tail.

In the weeks that followed this one-sided clash, Yokohama Kokutai, with half of its force in the Marshall Islands and half in Rabaul, flew daily patrols over its assigned sectors. The Rabaul detachment made two night raids on Port Moresby on 2–3 and 4–5 February. During the first mission, three (some sources say six or eight) H6K4s took off at 1900 hrs, arriving over the town at around 0130 hrs (Japanese Standard Time). The flying boats bombed from 12,000 ft, with one aircraft dropping illumination flares. Despite the presence of the latter, little damage was done – one militiaman was killed. On the second raid, five flying boats dropped some 50 bombs, destroying a store and damaging several buildings.

At around this time, the IJN received intelligence that another US Navy task force had left Pearl Harbor and was planning an attack on Wake Island or the South Seas area. Yokohama Kokutai duly received orders on 18 February to send four flying boats from its base in the Marshall Islands to Wake Island,

The US Navy carrier fighter was the nemesis of the IJNAF flying boat crews. Lt Cdr John Thach, flying the F4F-3 in the foreground, commanded VF-3 in the early carrier strikes in the Pacific and later at Midway, and shared in the destruction of a 'four-engined patrol bomber' (a Yokohama Kokutai H6K4) with his wingman, Ens Edward Sellstrom, on 20 February 1942. During 1942 US Navy Wildcat pilots would claim 17 Japanese flying boats shot down (*80G-10613, RG80, NARA*)

from where it was to fly long-distance patrol missions. The unit's flying boats at Rabaul were ordered to carry out patrols to the east of New Ireland.

On 19 February, two flying boats at Wake were sent on patrol, with another H6K4 heading out from Makin and two from Rabaul. The next day, Yokohama Kokutai instructed the Rabaul detachment to sortie three flying boats to cover sectors between 75 and 155 degrees to the east of Rabaul. The first H6K4 left Rabaul at 0430 hrs, the second departed at 0600 hrs and the third at 1200 hrs. None would return.

They were searching for TF 11, under the command of Vice Adm Wilson Brown, which included USS *Lexington* (CV-2). On 20 February the vessels were sailing parallel to Bougainville on a northwesterly course, planning to mount a surprise raid on Rabaul. At 1030 hrs Lt(jg) Noboru Sakai, the pilot of the first H6K4 to head out on patrol, radioed Rabaul that he had sighted the American force and gave its course. Locating the snooper on radar, *Lexington* sent off Lt Cdr John Thach, commanding officer (CO) of VF-3, and his wingman, Ens Edward Sellstrom, to intercept.

The H6K4 was flying in and out of cloud, but the two Wildcat pilots spotted the flying boat when it broke into clearer skies. Thach made a high-side run, firing at the starboard engines and puncturing a fuel tank. Coming in for a second attack, Thach approached from the right and Sellstrom from the left. Under their combined fire, the entire wing burst into flames and the H6K4 crashed into the sea.

Shortly thereafter, *Lexington* detected another snooper – the H6K4 flown by WO Kiyoshi Hayashi, which had been the second flying boat to take off from Rabaul. VF-3's Lt(jg) Bruce Stanley Jr and his wingman Ens Leon Hayes went out to intercept, and they found the silver-coloured flying boat 20 miles ahead of their carrier. In his book *The First Team – Pacific Naval Air Combat from Pearl Harbor to Midway*, John Lundstrom provided the following passage from Stanley's diary describing his attack;

'From above and behind this time as the broad wing filled the gunsight, the guns responded to the switch. The red trail of tracers could be seen to end abruptly as they passed from sight into the wing and the pilot compartment. Another burst, longer and more accurate now, and flame burst from the inboard engine on the port side. It disappeared and reappeared as I fired once more before ducking to avoid the tail. I looked back to see it become a solid sheet of flame from the wing to the fuselage. Gray smoke traced the path of the plane as the left wing and nose began to drop.'

As would continue to happen, the H6K4's unprotected fuel tanks caused the death of its crew. The flying boat crashed into the sea in a pall of smoke and flame. Although the pilots of VF-3 only claimed two H6K4s shot down, the third flying boat that left Rabaul that morning with Sub Lt Motohiro Makino as pilot also failed to return.

Early the next morning, six H6K4s took off from Rabaul at 0400 hrs for an attempted night torpedo attack on TF 11, but they could not locate the US Navy warships.

On 24 February, north of Rabaul, Adm Halsey's TF 16, with *Enterprise* as its centrepiece, launched an attack on Wake Island. Yokohama Kokutai had four flying boats on the island at the time, three of which were serviceable. Early in the morning the flying boats were alerted to the approach of enemy aircraft and hurriedly took off.

CPO Shohei Iwata was flying five miles east of Wake when F4Fs attacked his flying boat. He radioed that he was engaged in battle, but nothing more was heard from him. Flying at 15,000 ft, above Iwata, Lt Cdr Clarence Wade McClusky, CO of VF-6, led his division of four fighters down on the hapless flying boat. On his first pass, McClusky set the left outboard engine on fire. His wingman, Radio Electrician's Mate Edward Bayers, followed, setting another engine on fire. Lt Roger Mehle, leading the second section, was next, but as he closed on the flying boat and opened fire, the H6K4's fuel tanks exploded, forcing him to break away. The pilots of the remaining two flying boats avoided the American fighters and skilfully shadowed TF 16 until late afternoon.

For the remainder of February and through March Yokohama Kokutai flying boats flew patrols from Rabaul covering the Solomon Islands chain and New Guinea, and from Imieji and Wake out over the Central Pacific.

The most important mission during this time was Operation *K*, the second attack on Pearl Harbor. The Kawanishi Type 2 flying boat had by then completed its flight testing and been formally accepted into the IJNAF as the H8K1 Type 2 Flying Boat, Model 11. Several pre-production examples were assigned to Yokosuka Kokutai, where their impressive range of close to 4000 miles stimulated the idea that the H8K1 could be used for an attack on Pearl Harbor from the Marshall Islands, with a refuelling stop along the way. The headquarters of the Combined Fleet worked up a plan, designated Operation *K*, involving several H8K1s and submarines for refuelling.

On 25 January 1942, the 24th Koku Sentai Chief of Staff came to Tokyo to meet with the IJN General Staff and with Adm Yamamoto, commander of the Combined Fleet, who gave Yokohama Kokutai responsibility for carrying out the operation using H8K1 flying boats and crews from Yokosuka Kokutai. The mission would depart from Wotje, with refuelling taking place at French Frigate Shoals some 1605 miles from Wotje. The flying boats would then head for Pearl Harbor, 560 miles distant, before returning directly to Wotje, 1980 miles from Pearl Harbor. The operation was scheduled for early March. The initial idea was to employ five H8K1s, but only two – the third and fifth aircraft built – could be made available.

On 14 February, the aircraft, coded Y-71 and Y-72, reached Jaluit under the command of Lt Toshio Hashizume, an experienced flying boat pilot. The crews spent the next three weeks in training, twice practising refuelling

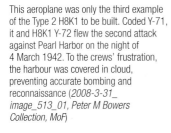

This aeroplane was only the third example of the Type 2 H8K1 to be built. Coded Y-71, it and H8K1 Y-72 flew the second attack against Pearl Harbor on the night of 4 March 1942. To the crews' frustration, the harbour was covered in cloud, preventing accurate bombing and reconnaissance (*2008-3-31_ image_513_01, Peter M Bowers Collection, MoF*)

from submarines at sea, flying nocturnal navigation exercises and bombing at night. With their training completed, the crews flew the two flying boats to Wotje on 2 March to wait for the day of the mission, scheduled for the 4th. Departing from Wotje, 250 miles to the north of Jaluit, would save three hours of flying time.

On 3 March Yokohama Kokutai sortied an H6K4 on a weather reconnaissance flight that ranged some 700 miles out from Wotje. Determining that the weather would be good, with a slight chance of cloud cover over Pearl Harbor, the mission went ahead. At 0025 hrs on 4 March, Y-71 took off with Lt Hashizume at the controls, followed by Y-72, flown by Ens Shosuke Sasao. The two flying boats followed long-wave radio signals from the submarine I-9 and reached French Frigate Shoals at 1300 hrs, circling for 50 minutes until the vessel surfaced. Despite difficult sea conditions, both aircraft took on 12,000 litres (3170 gallons) of fuel and took off again at 1600 hrs for Pearl Harbor.

They arrived over Oahu at 2110 hrs, only to find their target obscured by cloud cover. Hashizume approached the harbour on a bearing from a light house at Kaena Point, and when over it the clouds cleared and he spotted what he thought was Ford Island. Quickly turning his aircraft around, he dropped his bombs where he estimated his target to be. Sasao also had to bomb by estimating his position. Neither aeroplane's ordnance did any damage.

During the return flight, Hashizume's crew found that the hull of their aircraft had been damaged taking off from French Frigate Shoals, so they decided to land back at Jaluit because it had better maintenance facilities. Sasao landed at Wotje as planned. The two flying boats had spent 32 hours in the air.

Although a second attack was called off, Combined Fleet headquarters ordered Yokohama Kokutai to use the two flying boats to carry out a reconnaissance of Midway and Johnston Islands – both of interest for future operations. At 2150 hrs on 10 March, Lt Hashizume took off from Wotje in Y-71 to reconnoitre Midway, followed by Ens Sasao in Y-72, who would fly to Johnston Island. Sasao came within 15 miles of Johnston and made a thorough reconnaissance, returning to Wotje at 1440 hrs. Hashizume was not so fortunate.

As he approached Midway, radar on the island picked up his flying boat when it was 43 miles away and four F2A-3 fighters from VMF-221 were scrambled to intercept the approaching aircraft. Orbiting 20 miles off Midway, Capt James Neefus saw the flying boat five miles away from him flying at 9000 ft. As his gunners warned Hashizume of the approaching American fighters, he turned his aircraft away and went into a steep dive to gain speed. With the H8K1 attaining 276 mph as it descended for the water, the F2As struggled to close on the diving flying boat. Neefus eventually made a firing pass, followed by his wingman, 2Lt Francis McCarthy.

The second section also made firing passes, during which return fire from the flying boat hit GSgt Robert Dicky's aeroplane, wounding him in the arm. Seeing the flying boat enter clouds, Neefus waited for the H8K1 to emerge. Eventually, he too dived under the cloud layer and found a large fire on the water, with smoke and flames rising from where Hashizume's flying boat had crashed into the sea.

CHAPTER THREE

FLYING BOAT KOKUTAI APRIL–DECEMBER 1942

This early-build H6K5 from an unknown Kokutai is carrying a load of 60 kg bombs on the racks attached to the wing struts. Yokohama Kokutai made several bombing raids against Wake Island in the first weeks of the war, and later in the South Pacific, with limited results. A total of 36 H6K5s were built during the course of 1942, bringing overall production of the maritime reconnaissance version of the aircraft to 175 – a further 40 unarmed transport H6Ks were also completed (*20008-3-31_image_507_01, Peter M Bowers Collection, MoF*)

After an intense debate between the IJA and the IJN over the direction the next phase of operations should take, the Japanese Imperial General Headquarters (IGHQ) agreed on a series of offensives that it believed would allow the nation to retain the initiative in the Pacific War.

The success of the first phase of the Southern Operation had been beyond all expectations. Japanese forces had captured all objectives in Southeast Asia and the Pacific well within specified target dates. The goals of the second phase of operations were to maintain the momentum of success in order to pressure the Allies into making a negotiated settlement with Japan, expand Japan's defensive perimeter across the Pacific, and to bring the US Navy's fleet into a decisive battle where its inevitable defeat would hasten negotiations to end the war.

The first stage of operations called for the seizing of Port Moresby and Tulagi, in the Solomons, in a campaign codenamed Operation *MO*, thus securing Japan's hold on Rabaul. This would be followed by Operation *RY*, the capture of Narau and Ocean Islands to extend Japan's reach in the Pacific. The most ambitious operations were *AL*, to seize a foothold in the Aleutian Islands to guard the northern approaches to Japan, and *MI* to seize Midway Island. The IJNAF's flying boat units would play only a minor and short-lived role in *AL*, but they would be heavily involved in *MO*, and the protracted battle for Guadalcanal, in the Solomon Islands, that followed.

It appears that even before the IJN had finalised the second phase plans for the Southern Operation, it recognised the need for a third flying boat Kokutai. By the beginning of April 1942, Toko Kokutai was covering an area from Timor to the Indian Ocean, while Yokohama Kokutai was split between patrolling the Central Pacific, the Solomons and New Guinea out of Rabaul. *MO* would likely place even greater demands on Yokohama Kokutai, but there remained the need for active patrols over the Central Pacific.

The IJNAF activated 14th Kokutai on 1 April at Imieji by combining Yokohama Kokutai's six H6K4s split between there and at Makin with four H6K4s from Toko Kokutai based at Koepang. These aircraft flew from Koepang to Imieji via Ambon, Palau and Truk, arriving on 14 April. Four more H6K4s were assigned to Imieji, but on the flight from Truk on 27 April they ran into bad weather and had to make forced landings some distance from Jaluit. Emergency searches found one of the crews 40 miles south of Jaluit. The crew was rescued and, astonishingly, the rear half of the H6K4's fuselage was cut off and the front half towed back to Imieji. The other flying boats were never found.

14th Kokutai began patrol missions on 1 April using flying boats transferred from Yokohama Kokutai operating from Imieji and Makin. The new unit was formally established on 5 May after the arrival of personnel from Toko Kokutai.

At the same time, Eleventh Koku Kantai was reorganised and its flying boat Kokutai reallocated. Two new units, 25th Koku Sentai (Air Flotilla) and 5th Kushu Butai (Air Attack Force), were activated to coordinate

Yokohama Kokutai flight crews prepare for a mission from Rabaul's Simpson Harbour in May 1942. From a launch alongside, groundcrew help load the 7.7 mm Type 92 machine guns onto the flying boat (*P20000826dd1dd4phj838000 Mainichi Newspapers*)

naval air units and air operations from Rabaul over the Solomons and New Guinea. Koku Sentai were administrative units while Kushu Butai were purely tactical. 25th Koku Sentai and 5th Kushu Butai combined Tainan Kokutai (A6M Zero-sens) with 4th Kokutai (G4Ms) and Yokohama Kokutai, which was also given a detachment of A6M2-N floatplane fighters (the operations of the detachment are outside the scope of this volume).

The new 14th Kokutai replaced Yokohama Kokutai in 24th Koku Sentai, linked with 4th Kushu Butai, which returned to Eleventh Koku Kantai from Fourth Koku Kantai. Toko Kokutai remained with 21st Koku Sentai, linked with 1st Kushu Butai. 24th Koku Sentai and 4th Kushu Butai retained responsibility for the defence of the Marshall, Wake and Gilbert Islands. 21st Koku Sentai and 1st Kushu Butai were attached to the Southwest Area Fleet, where Toko Kokutai was assigned to the Malaya Unit and charged with patrolling the Indian Ocean and protecting the sea lanes to Rangoon. In addition, Toko Kokutai would contribute to the Northern Force operations from Honshu, in northern Japan. The new 25th Koku Sentai and 5th Kushu Butai would cover the Bismarcks, the Solomon Islands and New Guinea, and prepare for *MO*.

Tulagi, the capital of the British Solomon Islands, was the first objective of *MO*. It would provide a useful base for operations further south towards New Caledonia. The RAAF had established a radio station on a nearby island and was using the anchorage for its Catalina flying boats. To prepare for capturing Tulagi, Japanese forces occupied Buin, at the southern tip of Bougainville mid-way between Rabaul and Tulagi, in early April and started construction of a seaplane base on the Shortland Islands opposite Buin. At the end of the month Yokohama Kokutai H6K4s flew materials to the Shortland Islands to aid construction, and they soon began flying patrols from the base.

During the latter half of April the Kokutai flew daily patrols over the Solomons and towards New Guinea. The flying boats operating from the new Shortlands base contributed to attacks on Tulagi, with two bombing missions on 30 April (one in the morning and one in the early afternoon) seeing 250 kg and 60 kg bombs expended and 20 mm rounds fired from tail turret guns during strafing passes. The flying boats bombed Tulagi again on 2 May, and Japanese forces invaded the town and quickly occupied the RAAF radio station the following day.

That same day a Yokohama Kokutai H6K4 on patrol clashed with two US Army Air Force (USAAF) B-25 Mitchells from the 3rd Bombardment Group (BG) flying over the Solomon Sea between Port Moresby and Bougainville. As the bomber crews neared Bougainville, they sighted the Rabaul-based H6K4 flown by Cdr Saburo Shodo that was patrolling the same area. As he closed on the flying boat, 1Lt James Smith, flying one of the B-25s, found that neither of his powered turrets were working. Unperturbed, he ordered the bombardier to fire at the H6K4 with the 0.30-cal machine gun in the nose.

Smith and 2Lt Henry Rose in the other B-25 engaged the flying boat in a running fight lasting 35 minutes, making repeated head-on passes until 20 mm fire from the flying boat's tail turret damaged Smith's Mitchell and he had to break off the fight. The H6K4 returned to Rabaul with one crewman killed and several wounded.

A strike on Tulagi on 4 May alerted the Japanese to the presence of American carriers near the Solomons. This was TF 17, with *Yorktown* and *Lexington*. The Port Moresby invasion force was nearing Rabaul, with support from the 5th Carrier Division's *Shokaku* and *Zuikaku*, while the light carrier *Shoho* accompanied the invasion transports. Both sides sent out patrols to locate the opposing carrier forces in what became the Battle of the Coral Sea – a costly action for Yokohama Kokutai.

Before dawn on 5 May, Yokohama Kokutai sent off three flying boats from its base in the Shortlands to search for the American carriers. As Lt Kiyonosuke Urada's flying boat neared a point 30 miles from *Yorktown*, sailing south of the Solomon Islands in the Coral Sea, the carrier's radar detected the H6K4 and scrambled Lt Vincent McCormack's division of four F4F fighters from VF-42.

McCormack spotted the flying boat 25 miles from the carrier, Urada flying low at 700 ft above the water. Lt(jg) Arthur Brassfield, leading the second section, made the first attack, coming in from the right. McCormack then came in from the left, and as he pulled up from his pass two of the flying boat's engines were on fire. McCormack's wingman, Ens Walter Haas, followed his leader. Soon, all four of the Type 97's engines were burning, with flames spreading to the centre section of the wing. The doomed flying boat dived into the sea, its destruction having taken just 30 seconds.

Yokohama Kokutai sent out eight flying boats from the Shortlands and Tulagi on 6 May, and one of five H6K4s that took off from the latter site spotted TF 17 in the Coral Sea at mid-morning. Its crew maintained contact until mid-afternoon, sending out repeated reports. The next morning, four flying boats departed Tulagi just before dawn to continue the search. *Lexington*'s radar tracked one of the snoopers and vectored a section from *Yorktown*'s VF-42 onto the approaching flying boat. Lt Richard Crommelin led his wingman, Ens Richard Wright, into the attack, but Lt Isamu Sakamoto, pilot of the H6K4, entered cloud cover just after the US Navy fighters commenced a beam attack.

What followed was a combat that Crommelin noted closely 'compared to dogfighting tactics, as maneuvers were of a necessity very radical'. He and Wright made numerous runs from a short distance in and out of the overcast, firing bursts (Crommelin expended 1200 rounds) as Sakamoto tried to manoeuvre away from his attackers. Eventually, the cloud cleared, and the two F4Fs attacked again, Wright from the rear and above and Crommelin from above and to the left side. The H6K4 erupted in a ball of flame as its fuel tanks exploded.

On 8 May, as the rival carrier forces launched strikes against each other on the final day of the Coral Sea battle, Yokohama Kokutai lost another H6K4. Three flying boats had taken off on patrol from Tulagi before dawn, searching for TF 17. One crew had found the US Navy warships, which were already alerted to incoming 'bogeys'. Lookouts on *Yorktown* spotted the H6K4, and a few minutes later VF-42's Lt Vincent McCormack and his wingman, Ens Walter Haas, began their second attack on a Japanese flying boat in three days. McCormack made his first attack from above and to the right, following this with another high-side run from the left and a final pass from the right. Haas duplicated his attacks. The flying boat's engines started to smoke after the F4Fs made their first pass, and burst into flames as Haas commenced his final attack.

More H6K4s might have actually been lost, for on 7 and 8 May Yokohama Kokutai received orders to prepare for torpedo attacks on the American carriers at dusk. Luckily for the crews involved, the proposed attacks had to be cancelled on both days due to the IJNAF losing sight of the enemy vessels in bad weather on the 7th and concerns about possibly mistaking IJN carriers for American ones in a dusk attack. Immediately after the carrier clashes on 8 May, the Port Moresby invasion convoy was ordered to return to Rabaul. Two days later, the Combined Fleet postponed the Port Moresby invasion until at least July and ordered the 5th Carrier Division and its battered air groups to withdraw.

The focus now turned to Operations *MI* (the capture of Midway) and *AL* (the capture of positions in the Aleutians). In preparation for the attack on Midway, Adm Yamamoto needed to locate the remaining US Navy carriers in the Pacific – the Japanese assumed, erroneously, that they had sunk both *Lexington* and *Yorktown* in the Coral Sea clash, when only the former had in fact been lost. It was decided to use the new H8K1 flying boats once again to conduct a reconnaissance over Pearl Harbor, using submarines to refuel at French Frigate Shoals.

Since the beginning of the year Kawanishi had completed four H8K1s. The IJNAF allocated two of these early-production flying boats to 14th Kokutai for the Hawaii mission. Coded W-45 and W-46 to identify them as belonging to 14th Kokutai, they arrived at Imieji on 15 May. The mission was planned for the night of 30 May, but when the first refuelling submarine arrived at French Frigate Shoals it found a US Navy destroyer converted into a seaplane tender in the area. Instead of departing, the vessel was joined a few days later by a second destroyer-cum-seaplane tender. The mission was postponed to 31 May, but then PBY Catalinas alighted at French Frigate Shoals, forcing the commander of Eleventh Koku Kantai to cancel the mission.

14th Kokutai instead received orders to continue regular patrols to the east and to prepare to advance to Wotje and then on to Midway once the island had been captured. The subsequent heavy defeat of the IJN in Operation *MI* stalled any hope of advancing the Kokutai's flying boats. One of the H8K1s undertook a long sector search from Wake Island, flying some 1726 miles north-northeast of Wotje towards Midway and then covering 1381 miles on the return flight to Wake Island, the crew spending more than 18 hours in the air. The H8K1s flew several more patrols from Wotje until 19 June, when 14th Kokutai received orders to send the two H8K1s to Rabaul for operations in that area. Meanwhile, the unit's H6K4s spent the rest of June, July and August flying uneventful patrols over the Central Pacific sectors from Imieji and Makin.

OPERATION *AL*

Japanese forces landed on Kiska, an island in the Aleutian chain, on 7 June. The next day, six H6K4s from Toko Kokutai flew directly from Paramushir, in the Kurile Islands, to Kiska Harbor on the northwest shore of the island. The freighter *Kamitsu Maru* brought supplies and fuel for the flying boat detachment. The H6K4s immediately began flying patrols out to a distance of 345 miles searching for enemy shipping. Reconnaissance was difficult due to the notoriously poor weather in the Aleutians. When the flying boats went off on patrol, they faced unpredictable conditions upon their return to Kiska (as did the US Navy PBYs operating in the Aleutians). The IJNAF had intended to use the flying boats for long-range reconnaissance missions between Kiska and Midway, after its capture.

The IJNAF sent a detachment of 14 Type 0 Reconnaissance Seaplanes (E13A1s) to Kiska to operate alongside the Toko Kokutai detachment of H6K4s. This press photograph of a flight leader briefing crews before a sortie shows the rough conditions synonymous with operations in the Aleutians. The blurred outline of an H6K4 can just be made out in the upper left of the photograph (*Author's Collection*)

While on Kiska the flying boats flew several bombing missions against US Navy seaplane tenders serving the PBY squadrons in the Aleutians. On 20 July 1942, one of three H6K4s on a patrol sighted a seaplane tender in Kuluk Bay, on the island of Adak. The pilot of the flying boat suggested that the three aircraft return to Kuluk Bay at the end of their patrol to attack the vessel, USS *Gillis* (AVD-12), a converted destroyer. The three H6K4s bombed the seaplane tender in section formation but failed to inflict any damage.

The next day three flying boats flew to Nazan Bay on Atka Island but found no seaplane tender, so they dropped their twelve 250 kg bombs on the village nearby without observing any results due to cloud cover. Three H6K4s returned to Nazan Bay on 4 August, attacking the seaplane tender USS *Casco* (AVP-12) and the destroyer USS *Kane* (DD-235), but failed to damage either ship.

By now fully aware of the risk IJNAF aircraft posed to its vessels operating in the Aleutians, the US Navy had requested that the USAAF's 54th Fighter Squadron (FS) send out newly arrived P-38E Lightnings to patrol over Nazan Bay. On 9 August, a B-17 Flying Fortress escorted 1Lts Kenneth Ambrose and Stanley Long to the area, and as the bomber departed, it radioed both pilots to tell them that three Japanese flying boats were headed for Atka Island.

Having climbed to 22,000 ft above the bay, Ambrose and Long soon saw the three H6K4s some 15,000 ft below them. On spotting the American fighters diving down, the flying boats descended into the undercast below them. Ambrose and Long made two passes at the flying boats, with the former being certain he had set the wing of one of the H6K4s on fire. The P-38 pilots then flew on towards Kiska, where they found another flying boat – possibly the one they had attacked earlier – and made a firing pass before the aircraft disappeared into the clouds.

Ambrose and Long each received credit for shooting down a flying boat, with these being the first claims for the P-38 in World War 2. In fact, none of the H6K4s had been shot down, although one received damage to its tail. (*text continues on page 55*)

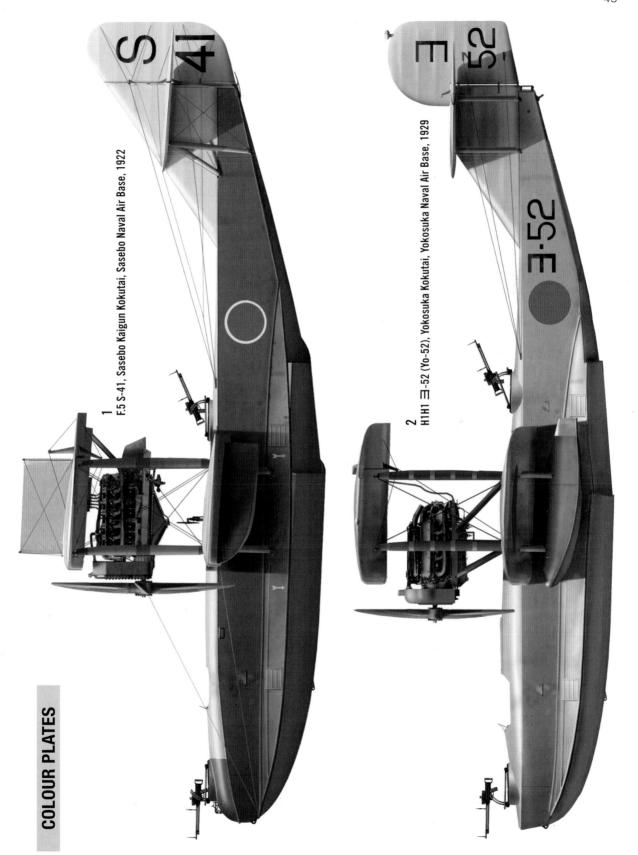

F.5 S-41, Sasebo Kaigun Kokutai, Sasebo Naval Air Base, 1922

2
H1H1 ヨ-52 (Yo-52), Yokosuka Kokutai, Yokosuka Naval Air Base, 1929

COLOUR PLATES

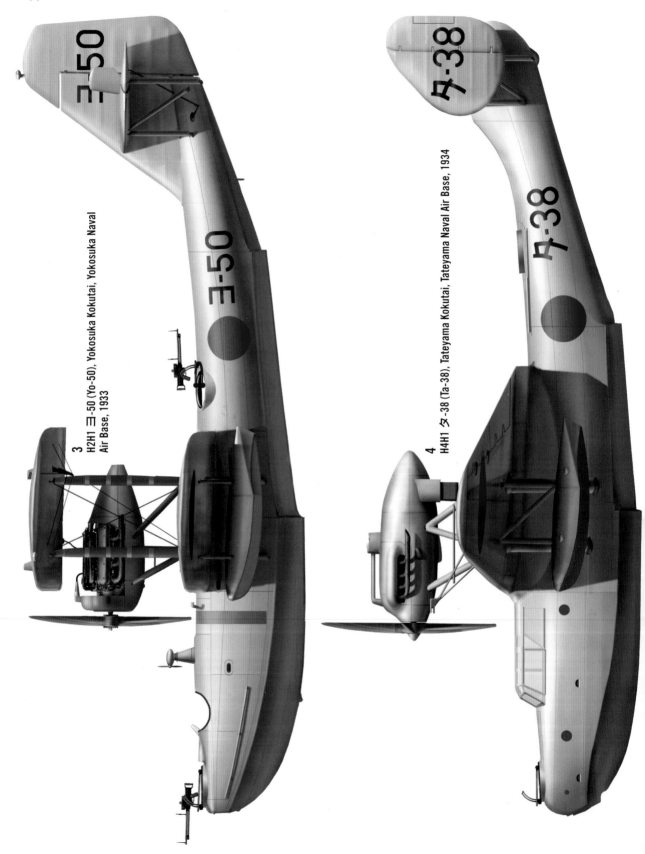

3
H2H1 ヨ-50 (Yo-50), Yokosuka Kokutai, Yokosuka Naval
Air Base, 1933

4
H4H1 夕-38 (Ta-38), Tateyama Kokutai, Tateyama Naval Air Base, 1934

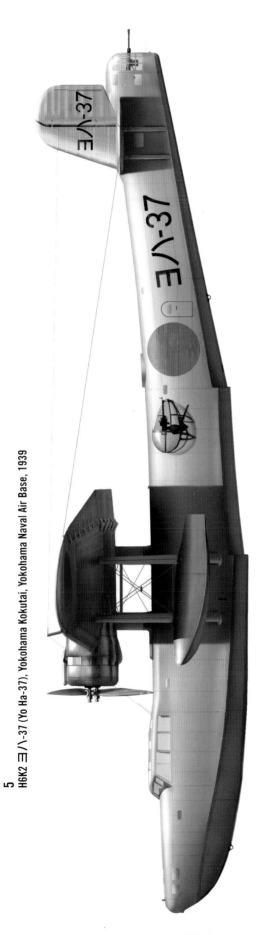

5
H6K2 ∃ノ八-37 (Yo Ha-37), Yokohama Kokutai, Yokohama Naval Air Base, 1939

6
H6K4 0-10, Toko Kokutai, Ambon, Netherlands East Indies, January–February 1942

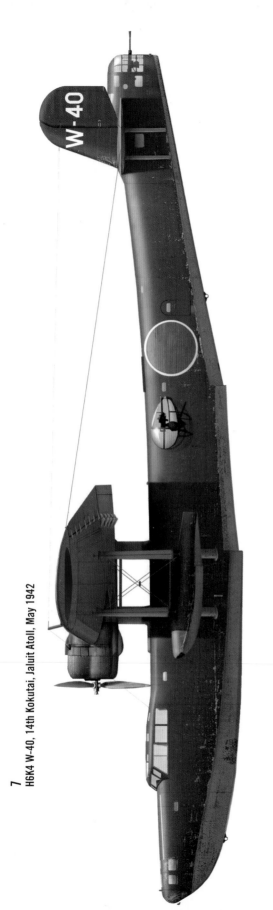

7
H6K4 W-40, 14th Kokutai, Jaluit Atoll, May 1942

8
H6K4 Y-44, Yokohama Kokutai, Rabaul, July 1942

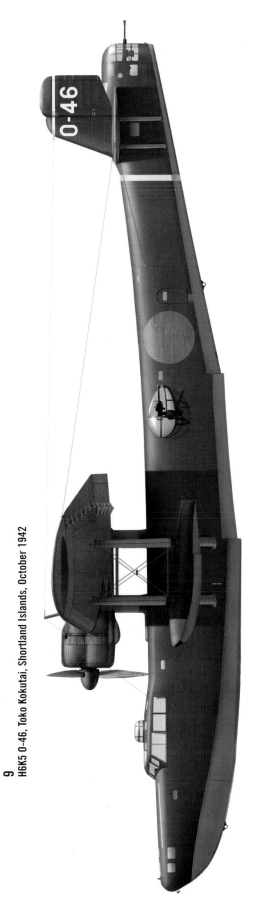

9
H6K5 0-46, Toko Kokutai, Shortland Islands, October 1942

10
H6K4 U3-30, 801st Kokutai, Horomushiro Naval Air Base, 1943

11
H6K5 N1-42, 802nd Kokutai, Jaluit, 1943

12
H6K5 タワ -66, Takuma Kokutai, Takuma Naval Air Base, 1944

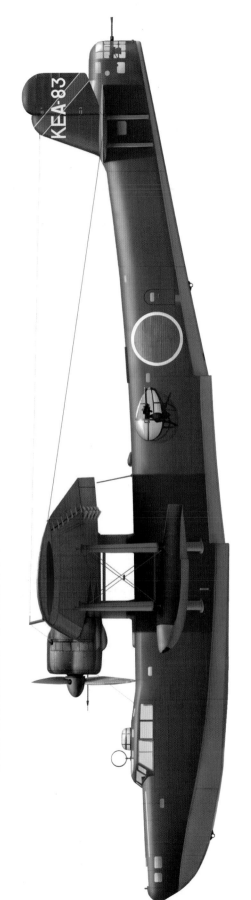

13
H6K5 KEA-83, 901st Kokutai, Toko, Formosa, early 1944

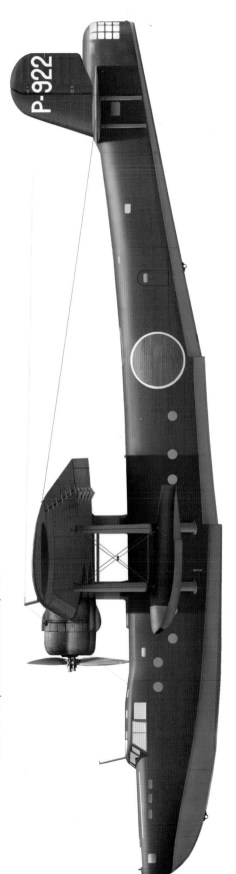

14
H6K4-L P-922, Eleventh Koku Kantai, 1943

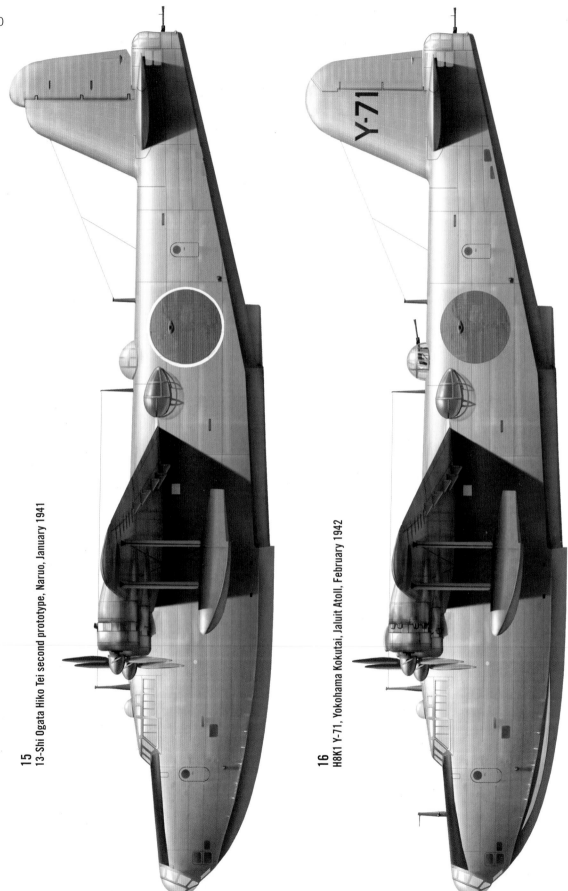

15
13-Shi Ogata Hiko Tei second prototype, Naruo, January 1941

16
H8K1 Y-71, Yokohama Kokutai, Jaluit Atoll, February 1942

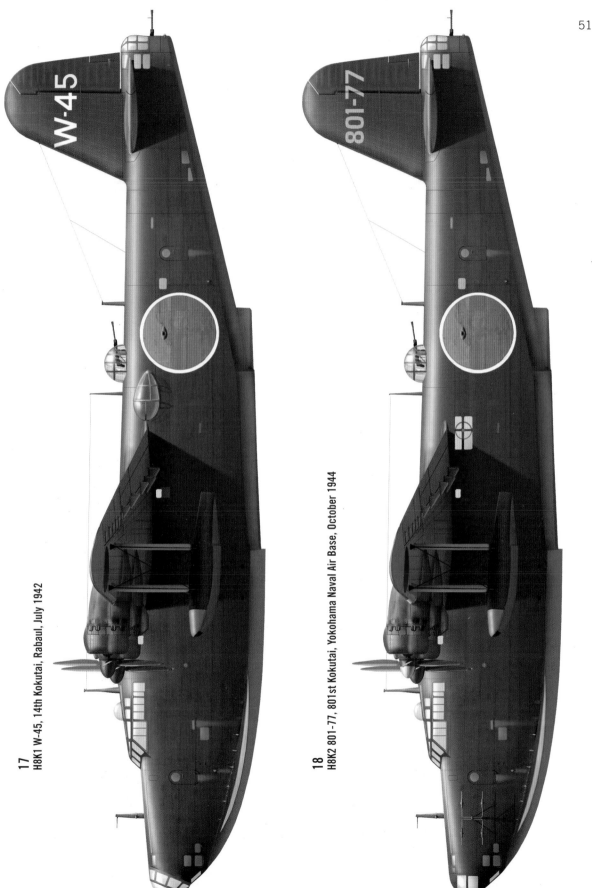

17
H8K1 W-45, 14th Kokutai, Rabaul, July 1942

18
H8K2 801-77, 801st Kokutai, Yokohama Naval Air Base, October 1944

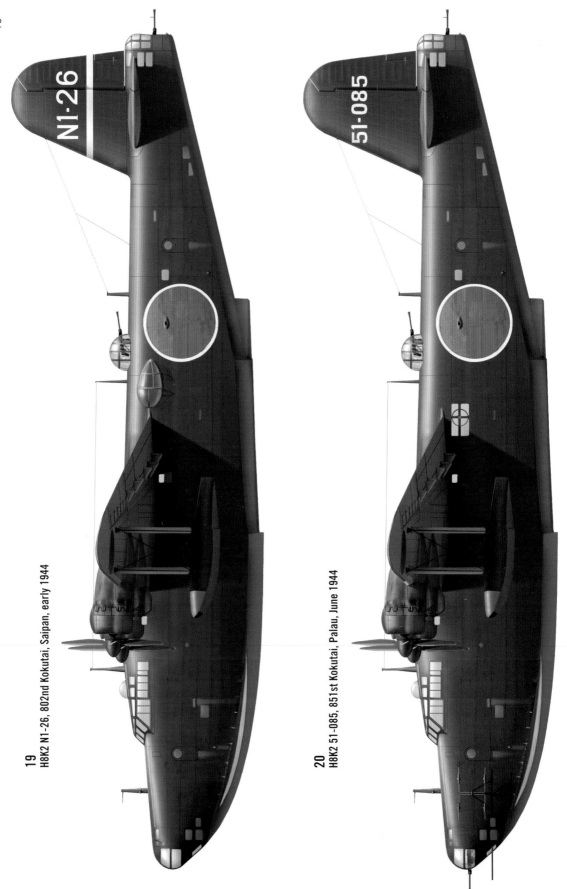

19
H8K2 N1-26, 802nd Kokutai, Saipan, early 1944

20
H8K2 51-085, 851st Kokutai, Palau, June 1944

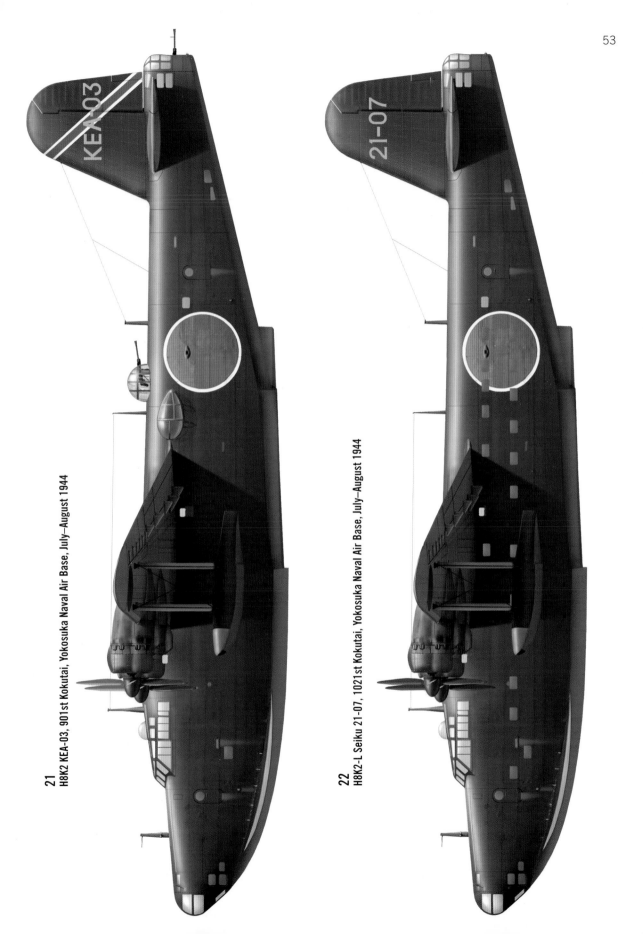

21
H8K2 KEA-03, 901st Kokutai, Yokosuka Naval Air Base, July–August 1944

22
H8K2-L Seiku 21-07, 1021st Kokutai, Yokosuka Naval Air Base, July–August 1944

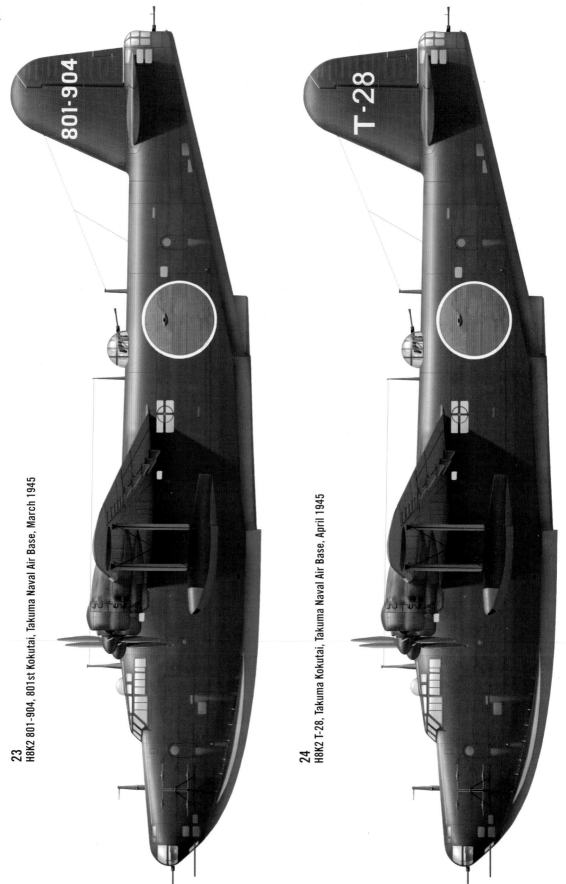

23
H8K2 801-904, 801st Kokutai, Takuma Naval Air Base, March 1945

24
H8K2 T-28, Takuma Kokutai, Takuma Naval Air Base, April 1945

This American reconnaissance photograph of Kiska Harbour, taken on 28 September 1942, shows the damage inflicted by gunfire from US Navy cruisers during the attack of 8 August. Four A6M2-N fighters can be seen in the lower left, eight E13A1 reconnaissance seaplanes in the centre and a sunken H6K4 flying boat in the upper right. Note also the incomplete seaplane ramp (80G-19970, RG80, NARA)

The Toko Kokutai detachment did not stay on Kiska much longer, having already lost two flying boats to operational causes by the time it ran into P-38s for the first time. One H6K4 disappeared on a return flight to Paramushir, while a second had to make a forced landing off Attu and sank, although the crew was rescued – these losses were made good with attrition replacements flown in from Japan. Just 24 hours prior to the clash with the Lightnings, US Navy light cruisers and destroyers shelled Kiska Harbor, sinking one H6K4 and damaging two more beyond repair. Realising the futility of continuing operations from there, the IJNAF ordered the three remaining flying boats back to Japan.

While their colleagues battled with fog and rain in the Aleutians, Toko Kokutai's flying boats continued patrolling the Indian Ocean from Port Blair and Penang. These were often long ten-hour missions searching for Royal Navy warships and Allied merchant vessels. Such sorties were monotonous, stressful and exhausting if flown day after day. Staring out at the vast expanse of ocean for hours on end, the crews had to remain vigilant. As in other maritime patrol forces, the IJNAF flying boat units usually flew a triangular patrol segment, flying out on one leg to the end of their patrol line, then turning left or right to fly a short leg to the return line. Crews would often see nothing at all, but not seeing anything could still provide vital information about the enemy.

When the IJNAF became aware that the aircraft carrier HMS *Formidable* had sortied from Ceylon at the beginning of August, Toko Kokutai sent out patrols from Port Blair to find the vessel and track its movements. On 2 August, one of four H6K4s that had sortied that day ran into two Fleet Air Arm Martlet fighters from *Formidable* some 30 miles east of the carrier. Like their US Navy colleagues, Sub Lts J E Scott and C Ballard made short work of Sub Lt Yokohama's H6K4.

During the rest of May, June and July, Yokohama Kokutai H6K4s at Rabaul, the Shortlands and Tulagi flew daily patrols over the Solomon

Islands chain, the seas to the east and west as far as Port Moresby and to the south towards Espiritu Santo. H6K4s also made a handful of early evening bombing attacks on Port Moresby. Three flying boats dropped thirty-six 60 kg bombs on Seven-Mile Drome on 25 May. Two more went out the following day and dropped twenty-four 60 kg bombs, with three returning on 27 May to drop six more bombs. The H6K4s made another evening raid on Port Moresby on 24 June, dropping thirty-six 60 kg bombs. None of these raids did any damage.

In June Yokohama Kokutai lost a flying boat to Allied aircraft. On the morning of the 11th, WO Kiyojo Yamaguchi had taken off from Rabaul to patrol over the Solomon Sea, but after several hours he had to turn back due to engine trouble. That same morning an RAAF Hudson from No 32 Sqn was also on patrol in overcast weather when, coming out of the clouds, its crew spotted a Japanese aircraft and identified it as a flying boat. Circling in the clouds, the Hudson dived down on the H6K4, with Plt Off Lex Halliday opening fire with his fixed 0.303-in machine guns in the nose before pulling up to give the Hudson's turret gunner a chance to fire. Halliday made several more passes, firing his guns at the hapless flying boat. The H6K4 hit the water seemingly attempting a forced landing, bounced, stalled and then crashed, at which point it burst into flames.

The month of July was noteworthy for the combat debut of the H8K1 in the South Pacific. 14th Kokutai received orders to send the two flying boats (both early-production H8K1s) it had on hand, W-45 and W-46, to Rabaul on 20 July for three weeks. They were to carry out reconnaissance missions over New Caledonia and Fiji and make night attacks on strategic bases in northeastern Australia. The H8K1 was the only Japanese aircraft that had the range for these missions. Up to this point the H8K1s had been reconnoitering the Gilbert and Ellice Islands.

The two H8K1s flew their first bombing mission to Australia on 25 July. Their targets were the wharves at Townsville and nearby Garbutt airfield, both in Queensland. Leaving Rabaul in the late afternoon, the two flying boats (one of which was flown by Lt Mizukura Kyoshi) arrived over Townsville just before midnight to be met with search lights. The flying boats dropped fifteen 250 kg bombs that landed in the water near the wharves, doing no damage. They returned to Rabaul early in the morning of 26 July after a flight of nearly 15 hours.

Two days later, H8K1 W-46 (flown by Lt Kyoshi) made a second attack, this time aiming for Garbutt airfield, dropping eight 250 kg bombs but missing the target. Six P-39 Airacobra fighters from the USAAF's 8th FG attempted an interception but failed to make contact. The next night (28 July), both H8K1s went out on what would be the last raid on Townsville. Although one flying boat had to return to Rabaul early, Lt Kingo Shoji in W-46 pressed on to the target. Radar had picked up his approach and four P-39s took off to intercept. When searchlights coned

On the night of 27–28 July 1942, Lt Mizukura Kyoshi of 14th Kokutai flew H8K1 W-46 from Rabaul to bomb Townsville. He arrived over the target and dropped his ordnance at 0215 hrs on 28 July. This was Kyoshi's second mission to Townsville in two days (*4093916, Australian War Memorial*)

the flying boat, Capts Robert Harriger and John Mainwaring made several firing passes, inflicting some damage on the H8K1 and forcing Shoji to jettison his bombs and descend rapidly to escape the searchlights and the fighters.

In the last few days of July the H8K1s flew two bombing missions against Horn Island off the tip of the Cape York Peninsula, in Queensland, where the RAAF had built an airfield, and against Cairns, north of Townsville. The first attack on Horn Island on the 29th damaged an RAAF Hudson, but during the second attack 48 hours later, 31 bombs dropped by the solitary H8K1 undertaking the raid fell harmlessly into the sea. During the attack on Cairns, a single H8K1 dropped bombs in error on the town of Mossman, north of Cairns, wounding a small child.

That same month, Capt Frank McCoy, an American intelligence officer attached to Allied Air Force, Southwest Pacific Area Headquarters, and his team began working on a simplified code system for quickly identifying IJAAF and IJNAF aircraft. The latter used the Type system as the primary means of designating its aircraft. Beginning in 1929, the Type number corresponded to the last two digits of the Japanese Imperial Year in which the IJNAF accepted the aircraft. Thus, the H6K was accepted in the Imperial Year 2597 (CE 1937 plus 660), being designated the Type 97 Flying Boat. This was the system used in IJNAF unit mission reports.

Japanese air- and groundcrews always referred to their aircraft using the Type system, usually with a nickname. The latter for flying boats was 'Tai Tei' ('Big Boat') – they would refer to the Type 97 Tai Tei or Type 2 Tai Tei.

The IJNAF also used what it called the 'short designation' system similar to the system the US Navy employed, which identified aircraft by function, a numeral indicating the number of aircraft in this function previously

F4F-4s from VF-71 take off from *Wasp* later in the day on 7 August 1942. Earlier that morning, the unit had attacked the IJNAF seaplane base at Tulagi along with SBD dive-bomber-equipped VS-71 and VS-5. Seven 'Mavis' flying boats of Yokohama Kokutai were anchored at nearby Tanambogo and three were in the water east of Tulagi, and they were all destroyed. Two more H6K4s at the Tulagi seaplane base escaped destruction by retreating to Rabaul just prior to the attack (*80G-14054, RG80, NARA*)

ordered, the manufacturer's initial and a second number indicating the model. Under the short designation system, the first Type 97 was designated the H6K1, indicating that it was the first model of the sixth Navy flying boat, built by Kawanishi.

The problem facing the Allies was that the IJNAF had several aircraft accepted in the year 2597, resulting in there being several Type 97s in frontline service. McCoy's team came up with simple American names – boys' names for fighters and floatplanes, girls' names for bombers, reconnaissance aircraft and flying boats – to identify Japanese aircraft. Since it was well known from pre-war publicity, the Type 97 flying boat was one of the first aircraft to receive a name under this system, becoming the 'Mavis'. When Allied intelligence became aware of a newer four-engined flying boat, initially identified as the Type 99 and later correctly as the Type 2 Flying Boat, it received the name 'Emily'. While it is more correct to identify IJNAF aeroplanes by their Type number, from here on the text will refer to the 'Mavis' and the 'Emily' as well, for these names are more familiar to Western readers.

In August the bitter and protracted battle for Guadalcanal began with the American invasion of the island on the 7th. During the first month of fighting the flying boat units would suffer heavy losses, so much so that Yokohama Kokutai had to be withdrawn back to Japan to rebuild the unit. Once again, carrier-borne fighters would inflict most of the losses, intercepting the H6K4s as they tried to locate and trail US Navy task forces near the Solomons. But 'Mavis' crews would also encounter USAAF B-17 bombers conducting reconnaissance missions. The aerial battles between the four-engined aircraft would sometimes end in a draw and sometimes in the loss of the 'Mavis'.

The seaplane base at Tanambogo Island, near Tulagi, comes under attack from SBDs of VS-71 and VS-5 on the morning of 7 August. Yokohama Kokutai not only lost seven flying boats but many air- and groundcrew in this surprise raid (80G-11899, RG80, NARA)

The transport vessels bound for Guadalcanal with the US Marine Corps' 1st and 2nd Marine Divisions embarked had the support of TF 61, including the carriers *Enterprise*, *Saratoga* and USS *Wasp* (CV-7).

In the pre-dawn darkness on 7 August, Lt Cdr Courtney Shands, CO of VF-71 flying from *Wasp*, led 11 F4F fighters to attack the seaplane base at Tulagi and the nearby islets of Gavutu and Tanambogo, where Yokohama Kokutai had stationed seven H6K4s. Four were anchored at Tanambogo and three were in the water east of Tulagi being fuelled for the morning's patrols. The VF-71 Wildcats made repeated passes, destroying all the flying boats and many Type 2 (A6M2-N 'Rufe') floatplane fighters. Immediately after VF-71 had finished strafing, SBD Dauntlesses from VS-71 and VS-5 bombed Tulagi's installations. Fortunately for Yokohama Kokutai, two H6K4s had taken off from there just prior to the attack, retreating safely to Rabaul.

For the next few days Yokohama Kokutai sent out patrols from Rabaul, searching to the east for the American task force. On 12 August two more H6K4s arrived from Saipan to make up losses, and the following day 14th Kokutai received orders to transfer three 'Mavis' flying boats to Rabaul for a ten-day deployment. These aircraft arrived on 18 August, joining two 'Emily' flying boats of Yokohama Kokutai that had been temporarily ordered to remain at Rabaul. These five aircraft duly made long-range reconnaissance flights to New Caledonia and beyond, spending nearly 18 hours in the air.

On 15 August Toko Kokutai also received orders to send a detachment of H6K4s to Rabaul. Six aircraft left Port Blair 13 days later, flying to Rabaul via Singapore, Saigon, Manila, Palau and Truk. Two more departed shortly thereafter. The detachment arrived at Rabaul on 2 September and flew its first patrol that afternoon.

For nearly two weeks following the debacle at Tulagi, H6K4 crews from Yokohama Kokutai and newly arrived 14th Kokutai flew their daily patrols over the Solomons and the seas to the east without interference. During the latter part of the month, however, both units suffered several losses to American aircraft.

The first encounter took place on 20 August when WO To'oru Ogawa, flying one of three Yokohama Kokutai H6K4s sent out on patrol, ran into a B-17E from the 11th BG's 98th Bombardment Squadron (BS) flown by Capt Walter Lucas near Santa Isabel Island north of Guadalcanal. The 'Mavis' passed the Flying Fortress while flying at 8000 ft, prompting Lucas to turn his bomber around and attack the flying boat from below. For 25 minutes the two aircraft exchanged gunfire in an aerial duel until the 'Mavis' caught fire. Ogawa made a landing near an atoll, from where he and his remaining crew were rescued nearly three weeks later.

Earlier that morning a 14th Kokutai 'Mavis' flown by WO Iwao Taguchi had spotted an enemy force comprising a cruiser and two destroyers, and an hour later it found an American carrier and its escorts. This was the escort carrier USS *Long Island* (ACV-1), delivering US Marine Corps F4F fighters and SBD dive-bombers to Guadalcanal. Taguchi continued to trail the carrier until an SBD from VS-71 on an ASW patrol spotted the 'Mavis' and gave chase. Taguchi broke off his reconnaissance, but not before exchanging fire with the SBD, his tail gunner hitting it with 20 mm rounds that forced Ens Harlan Coit to break off his attack. Taguchi was fortunate that a combat air patrol from VF-71 never caught up with him. In the early afternoon, another 14th Kokutai 'Mavis' sighted a different US Navy carrier force, alerting the Japanese command to its presence southeast of Tulagi.

On 21 August, 14th Kokutai H8K1s W-45 and Y-53 set off before dawn on a long-range search but found nothing. Yokohama Kokutai sent off three 'Mavis' flying boats from the Shortland Islands base at 0630 hrs local time and two more an hour later, searching to the southeast. Mid-morning, WO Yasuichi Tokunaga of Yokohama Kokutai reported five American ships, but 15 minutes later he came under attack from an SBD flown by Lt Robert Ware of VS-72, embarked in *Wasp*. Tokunaga flew into broken clouds, but Ware came after him. When the two aeroplanes broke into clear skies above the clouds, Ware closed in to within 50 ft of the 'Mavis', holding his trigger down. The SBD's two 0.50-cal machine guns set the port outer engine on fire, and the blaze soon spread to the fuel tanks. The left wing of the 'Mavis' burned off and the flying boat crashed into the sea. A frustrated fighter pilot from VF-71 wrote in his diary 'Wish the damn scouts would tend to their own business'.

On 22 August 14th Kokutai sent out two 'Mavis' flying boats from the Shortlands Islands base and a single 'Emily' from Rabaul to search for the American carriers. Five H6K4s from Yokohama Kokutai also sortied from the Shortland Islands to cover the same areas.

14th Kokutai crews would meet with ill fortune during the course of the day. Mid-morning, radar on *Enterprise* identified a 'bogey' 55 miles northwest of the carrier, which was sailing south of Guadalcanal. Unable to contact the combat air patrol (CAP) sent off earlier, *Enterprise* launched three more divisions of F4Fs. Lt Albert Vorse and his division received a vector and headed towards the 'bogey', climbing to 10,000 ft. They soon sighted the 'Mavis' flown by PO1c Shoichi Ogata, who apparently radioed that he was under attack as Vorse and his wingman, Ens Richard Loesch, barrelled in on him. Vorse opened fire first and sent 100 rounds into the 'Mavis', setting the wing and fuselage on fire. Loesch also fired at the flying boat, but by then the H6K4 was already burning fiercely. Minutes later the wing collapsed and the aircraft broke up.

To counter the American landings, the Japanese initiated Operation *Ka* to send a convoy of troops to Guadalcanal with a strong naval escort, including the carriers *Shokaku* and *Zuikaku* and the light carrier *Ryujo*. This move would result in a clash between US Navy and IJN carriers known as the Battle of the Eastern Solomons. On the morning of 24 August, the Japanese transports were still some 300 miles from Guadalcanal.

Both sides ordered extensive patrols to locate their carrier forces. Yokohama Kokutai sent out two H6K4s to search for the American carriers known to be in the area, while 14th Kokutai despatched two H8K1s, W-45 and Y-53 (the latter aircraft possibly being the first Type 2 assigned to Yokohama Kokutai although appearing in the 14th Kokutai mission report).

Commanding Y-53, WO Kiyomi Ata was flying on a line 122 degrees from the Shortlands when he saw F4Fs approaching his flying boat. *Saratoga* had picked up the aircraft on radar and vectored Lt David

Three H6K4s sit at their moorings in Rabaul's natural harbour in September 1942. Following the capture of Tulagi by the US Marine Corps in August, Toko and 14th Kokutai were forced to fly patrols over the Solomons and New Guinea from Rabaul and the Shortland Islands (*P2022908dd1dd3phj767000 Mainichi Newspapers*)

Richardson's division out to intercept it. Seeing the approaching F4Fs, Ata climbed several thousand feet before commencing a fast dive towards cloud cover below. In response to this manoeuvre, Richardson sent Lt(jg) Frank Green's section below the cloud layer while he and his wingman stayed above it.

Green saw the 'Emily' emerge from the clouds and radioed Richardson while he and his wingman made the first attack. Ignoring the fire from the flying boat's 20 mm dorsal turret Richardson also then attacked, followed by his wingman, Ens Foster Blair. They set the inboard port engine alight, forcing Ata to perform a steep wingover to the left which possibly caused the stall that sent the 'Emily' crashing into the sea. This was the first Type 2 flying boat that US Navy pilots had encountered, and as they were unfamiliar with the new aeroplane, they identified it as a 'Sikorsky S-44'.

14th Kokutai lost two more H8K1s in quick succession. On the second day of the battle (25 August) it sent out another 'Emily' with Ens Tatsuhisa Ito in command. He found TF 18, comprised of *Wasp* and its escorts, and shadowed the force for 40 minutes. The flying boat rashly flew too close to a VS-71 division of SBDs on patrol near *Wasp*, the Dauntlesses climbing above the 'Emily' and then diving down to attack it. Division leader Lt Morris Doughty made the first pass, setting fire to the flying boat's right inboard engine. Ito tried to escape by executing a chandelle, but the remaining three SBDs all attacked. With unprotected fuel tanks in the H8K1, the 'Emily' quickly exploded under the weight of fire from the dive-bombers.

Two days later, veteran 'Emily' W-45 of 14th Kokutai met its end. Just before dawn, Lt(jg) Chojiro Hayashi, who had commanded the unit's small flight of H8K1s, took off from Rabaul to search a sector 123 degrees to the southeast. Sending a warning of contact with enemy ships, Hayashi soon found himself under attack from a division of VF-71 fighters off *Wasp*. At 1435 hrs local time, he radioed that he was coming under fire. Ens David Senft, leading the division, came in on the 'Emily' from the right with his wingman, Ens Millard Thrash, while his other section, comprising Ens William Hall and Ens Earl Steiger, approached from the left. Hayashi made a tight left turn to avoid Senft and Thrash, but this put the 'Emily' right in front of Hall and Steiger, who opened fire and hit the flying boat's centre section. The unprotected fuel tanks burst into flames and the 'Emily's' wings folded up, after which the flying boat broke apart.

Yokohama Kokutai flew its last patrols over the Solomons during the first week of September, then withdrew back to Japan. By the end of August there were only four H6K4s serviceable at Rabaul. 14th Kokutai needed to retain them for operations in the Central Pacific, so it sent H8K1s to Rabaul in exchange.

Ten days after the landings on Guadalcanal, the US Marine Corps raided Makin Island. 14th Kokutai sent its H6K4s from Imieji to Makin to carry out reconnaissance, and they found the US Navy submarines that had carried the raiding party to Makin but did not attack. Following the attack on Makin, 14th Kokutai flew extensive searches in the area looking for American ships. At the end of August the unit sent three H6K4s to operate out of Makin in support of Operation *RY*. Throughout September, 14th Kokutai sent out H6K4s on daily patrols from Imieji and Makin, while the small detachment of two H8K1s flew from Rabaul.

During September, the Toko Kokutai H6K4 detachment flew most of the long-range patrols that were undertaken in-theatre, initially from Rabaul before moving to the Shortland Islands. As a result, the unit experienced all the encounters with Allied aircraft that month, claiming several shot down but also suffering losses at the hands of both US Navy and USAAF aircraft. The first encounter took place on 5 September when Lt(jg) Masa'aki Kuma clashed with a PBY Catalina from VP-11 420 miles east of the Shortland Islands. Lt(jg) Francis Riley and his crew set the 'Mavis' on fire, forcing Kuma to land on the water. He and his crew abandoned the flying boat as it sank, with little hope of rescue.

The next day, two H6K4s had run-ins with American aircraft while on patrol from the Shortlands. East of Bougainville, PO1c Sadao Kusano ran into another VP-11 PBY. The 'Mavis' crew exchanged fire with the PBY, firing twenty 20 mm rounds from the tail turret and twenty-two 7.7 mm rounds from the nose and waist guns. These were enough to kill the pilot of the PBY, Lt(jg) Charles Willis. The two flying boats then broke off the engagement and continued on their way. Elsewhere that same day, another 'Mavis' clashed with a Flying Fortress from the 11th BG, exchanging fire before escaping into clouds. The H6K4 crew fired 170 20 mm and 173 7.7 mm rounds, receiving 36 hits from the B-17E's 0.50-cal machine guns in return.

There were more encounters with Flying Fortresses on 7 and 8 September. On the 7th, 1Lt Charles Norton was the pilot of a 42nd BS/11th BG B-17E flying a reconnaissance mission when he encountered a 'Mavis' and attacked it. His gunners failed to damage the aircraft, and the H6K4 crew fired back and set the B-17's No 1 engine alight after hitting its oil tank. The next day, Lt(jg) Mitsuyoshi Suzuki was flying a 'Mavis' on patrol when he encountered another 42nd BS/11th BG B-17 near Rendova Island. Suzuki's crew fired 44 rounds of 20 mm and 1240 rounds of 7.7 mm ammunition at the bomber, causing it to crash on the island in a rare victory for the flying boat – possibly the first air-to-air victory of the war for the H6K4.

1Lt Norton and his crew had a second encounter with a 'Mavis' on 9 September. While on a reconnaissance mission 800 miles from their base on Espiritu Santo, he spotted the H6K4 flown by PO1c Shinzaku I'izuka on a similar patrol. The two aircraft exchanged fire, with the B-17's gunners scoring 25 hits on the 'Mavis' and their IJNAF counterparts expending 60 rounds of 20 mm ammunition, hitting the B-17's tail and both wings, and 500 7.7 mm rounds which struck the pilot's cockpit, the No 2 engine and the ball turret, wounding the gunner inside.

The next action between an IJNAF flying boat and American aircraft took place on 15 September, 48 hours after a 14th Kokutai detachment H8K1 sighted TF 61, which had been delivering aeroplanes to US Marine Corps units at Henderson Field, on Guadalcanal. Lt(jg) Kiyoshi Mizukura, who commanded the H8K1 detachment, came close enough to the vessels to identify and report the sighting without attracting fighter interception.

The next day Toko Kokutai sent out six H6K4s to search for the American carriers but they found nothing. On 15 September it sortied four H6K4s to the east of the Shortland Islands in search of an American task force that was escorting transport vessels to Guadalcanal. The Toko Kokutai mission report for that date indicates that one of the patrolling flying boats spotted what its crew identified as an enemy carrier, a seaplane carrier and, later, a group of transports.

Two flying boats also reported being attacked by enemy fighters, with the 'Mavis' flown by PO1c Senyu Katsumi firing forty-five 20 mm and three hundred and fifty 7.7 mm rounds and seeing one aeroplane shot down, while the other 'Mavis', flown by PO1c Maemura Tadayoshi, fired thirty 20 mm rounds and sixty-four 7.7 mm rounds. There are, however, no corresponding US Navy or USAAF reports of fighters engaging in a dogfight with these aircraft. A third 'Mavis', flown by Lt Shigeru Yoneyama, failed to return from the mission.

That morning *Hornet* and *Wasp* were providing cover for the transport vessels when the former's radar picked up a 'bogey'. *Wasp* was controlling the CAP, and it sent off a division of VF-71 F4Fs. When he saw the American fighters, Yoneyama tried to escape with a diving turn to the left, but Lt(jg) John McBrayer caught up with him and fired at the centre of the wing, causing the 'Mavis' to burst into flames.

Two H6K5s from an unknown Kokutai fly in close formation in late 1942. This 'Mavis' variant was equipped with Mitsubishi Kinsei 53 engines giving 1300 hp for take-off. The 36 examples built in 1942 went to Toko and Yokohama Kokutai as attrition replacements (01_00081856, San Diego Air and Space Museum (SDASM))

Toko Kokutai flying boats ended the month with two brief engagements involving B-17s from the 431st BS/11th BG. On 28 September 1Lt Sam White spotted a 'Mavis' approaching in the opposite direction at 1000 ft. He immediately turned and went in pursuit, slowly gaining on the flying boat. The pilot of the H6K4, PO2c Kamei Rin, dropped down to 100 ft above the water, and as the B-17 came after him he skilfully manoeuvred his aircraft so that the bomber always faced the flying boat's tail turret. With no speed advantage, White's B-17 never got closer than 800 yards from the 'Mavis'. Both aircraft exchanged fire, the H6K4 expending 135 rounds of 20 mm ammunition and 1500 7.7mm rounds, apparently without inflicting any damage on the bomber, before leaving the combat after 40 minutes with nine hits from the B-17's machine guns.

September ended with another brief exchange of fire between a B-17 and a Toko Kokutai 'Mavis' as they passed each other on patrol on the 30th.

October proved to be a difficult month for both flying boat units, which suffered losses to US Navy F4Fs and SBDs. The Japanese made a concerted effort to defeat American forces on Guadalcanal during the course of October, sending reinforcements to the island, employing battleships to bombard Henderson Field and mounting a series of air raids, before engaging the US Navy in the Battle of the Santa Cruz Islands at month-end, but all to no avail.

Although reduced to only five H6Ks by 30 September, and with just one H8K1 remaining from the 14th Kokutai detachment, Toko Kokutai continued flying daily patrols from Rabaul. In an effort to augment it, 14th Kokutai received orders to send four H6K4s to Rabaul by 9 October. Later in the month the unit was instructed to extend searches from Makin out some 700 miles to the southwest in the direction of the Solomon Islands.

Toko Kokutai lost two H6Ks searching for the American carriers. On 12 October, TF 17, with *Hornet*, was heading southwest of the Russell Islands when radar picked up a snooper. The carrier's Fighter Direction Officer (FDO) sent Lt(jg)s George Formanek and Richard Hughes from VF-72 off to intercept. They were flying at 13,000 ft when a 'Mavis' was spotted several thousand feet below them. This was the Toko Kokutai H6K

On 23 October 1942, 1Lt Edwin Loberg and his crew from the 26th BS/11th BG shot down a 14th Kokutai H6K4 in this B-17E, 41-2433, christened *Miss Fit* and camouflaged in the distinctive Hawaiian Air Depot scheme. Remarkably, a month later, this same Flying Fortress had another encounter with a 'Mavis', making multiple passes that resulted in both aircraft suffering damage. Note the underwing aerial for the SCR-521/ASV air-to-surface radar fitted to the aircraft (*USAF*)

flown by PO1c Fumio Kato. The two F4Fs came in from the right in a high-side pass, setting the port inboard engine on fire. As Kato entered a dive to escape, Formanek came in on a second high-side pass, setting the outboard port engine on fire. The flying boat's fuel tanks quickly exploded, sending the 'Mavis' down in flames.

Formanek and Hughes downed another 'Mavis' three days later after *Hornet* picked up a snooper on radar. WO Toshihito Yaguchi, also from Toko Kokutai, was on his way back to the Shortland Islands when the F4Fs appeared above him. As the H6K headed down for the water, Formanek and Hughes came in again on high-side runs from the left. Formanek then returned for a second pass from the right, closing to point-blank range. As Hughes began his second run, the 'Mavis' exploded.

Toko Kokutai lost another H6K on 16 October while searching for the American task force. On this day, Lt Yoshihiko Hinata, a unit *buntaicho* (section leader), found the US Navy warships 60 miles southeast of Guadalcanal. An SBD from VB-8 on inner air patrol spotted the flying boat and climbed to intercept. Lt(jg) Frank Christofferson made five passes on the 'Mavis', but 20 mm fire from the flying boat's tail turret damaged his SBD so badly he had to ditch.

Lt Thomas Johnson and his wingman, Ens Philip Souza, from VF-72 were descending from flying the high CAP when they learned of the 'bogey's' position. Souza spotted the 'Mavis' first and came in on a high-side run, followed by Johnson. After making three runs, Souza briefly lost the H6K in clouds, but he found it again in the clear and made a fourth pass on the flying boat. Squadronmate Lt(jg) Robert Jennings, flying the medium CAP, then joined Souza, and together their fire caused the 'Mavis' to erupt in flames and crash.

That same day, 14th Kokutai lost a 'Mavis' to a B-17 – the first of four the unit would have shot down by Flying Fortresses in just nine days. 1Lt Wayne Thompson from the 72nd BS/11th BG was flying a patrol east of Santa Isabel Island, northeast of Guadalcanal, when he and his crew saw an H6K and went in to attack. The 'Mavis' pilot, who was undertaking a patrol from Makin, flew into scattered clouds in an attempt to escape but they provided little in the way of cover. The B-17 gunners expended 3000 0.50-cal rounds to down the 'Mavis', while the flying boat gunners returned fire and a 20 mm round hit the ball turret, wounding the gunner inside.

Seven days later, on 23 October, the 26th BS/11th BG sent 1Lt Edwin Loberg out to patrol an area southwest of Guadalcanal in search of IJNAF flying boats. Loberg was at the controls of B-17E 41-2433, christened *Miss Fit* for all the damage it had received. Reaching the target area, Loberg flew a reconnaissance at 1000 ft and then climbed to 6000 ft, where he commenced circling. After an hour, one of the crew spotted a 'Mavis' approaching below. The 14th Kokutai H6K had taken off from the Shortland Islands base before dawn to patrol the area south of Guadalcanal, with PO2c Eto Tsuneo in command.

Loberg spiralled down in his B-17 and the gunners began firing, the 'Mavis' shooting back and trying to escape into clouds. At one point in the battle the Flying Fortress flew so close to the flying boat that the American gunners could see the Japanese crew. Heavily damaged, the 'Mavis' crashed into the water and exploded.

The 72nd BS/11th BG claimed another H6K east of Malaita Island on 24 October, PO2c Arishima Yoshiyuki and his crew being listed as unreturned. The following day, the 42nd BS/11th BG also claimed a 'Mavis' shot down during a search mission east of Santa Isabella Island, ending a bad month for 14th Kokutai.

On 1 November the IJNAF reorganised its land-based Kokutai based on a new system of numerical designations in place of base names. In the new three-digit system, the first digit indicated the type of aeroplane flown, the second digit the naval district the Kokutai was assigned to and the third digit

Lt Stanley 'Swede' Vejtasa and his VF-10 division claimed a 'Mavis' shot down 40 miles from their carrier, *Enterprise*, on the morning of 13 November 1942 during the Naval Battle of Guadalcanal. The next day, his squadronmates Lt Macgregor Kilpatrick and Lt(jg) William Blair also shared in the destruction of a 'Mavis'. Both flying boats were from 851st Kokutai, formerly Toko Kokutai. This would be the last US Navy carrier fighter claim for a Japanese flying boat until September 1943 (*80G-39610, RG80, NARA*)

identified the Kokutai itself. For flying boat and seaplane fighter units, the IJNAF chose numbers in the 800 range. The new designations for the flying boat units were 801st Kokutai (formerly Yokohama Kokutai), 802nd Kokutai (formerly 14th Kokutai) and 851st Kokutai (formerly Toko Kokutai).

There were also a few changes in assignments. 801st Kokutai, still rebuilding from its losses in the Solomons, remained a part of 25th Koku Sentai, based at Yokohama. However, responsibility for 851st Kokutai was transferred from 21st Koku Sentai to the Southwest Area Fleet, but the unit continued to maintain a detachment at Rabaul and the Shortland Islands. 802nd Kokutai was placed under Eleventh Koku Kantai control, although it remained with 4th Kushu Butai. The Kokutai was ordered to pull its flying boat detachment from Rabaul back to Imieji, leaving behind its Type 2 'Rufes' and, apparently, a single 'Emily'. This left the 851st Kokutai detachment as the only flying boat unit operating over the Solomons – despite the reorganisation, there was no interruption in its patrol duties from Rabaul and the Shortland Islands.

Believing that the remaining US Navy carriers had been eliminated during the Battle of the Santa Cruz Islands at the end of October, IGHQ initiated Operation *Z* in an effort to reinforce IJA troops of the Seventeenth Army on Guadalcanal and use IJN battleships to bombard Henderson Field. This led to the Naval Battle of Guadalcanal between 13–15 November. To support the Japanese attack, 851st Kokutai sent out patrols of three flying boats on 13 and 14 November and two on the 15th in search of US Navy vessels.

Two of these crews had the misfortune of running into F4Fs from VF-10, embarked in *Enterprise* (again part of TF 16), on the morning of 13 November. The carrier's radar picked up a 'bogey' approaching TF 16, and Lt Stanley 'Swede' Vejtasa and his division were given a vector to intercept. In his memoire Vejtasa recounted the action that followed their sighting of the 'Mavis';

'We watched him for ten miles; he's low down. I've got the throttle on full, and my division mates are creeping up on me, passing me, they've all got the power on. As we close I open fire, and the others do as well. After an extended bunch of confused runs and an unbelievable number of expended rounds, suddenly, God Almighty, there's nothing but a fantastic burst of smoke and fire. Under the combined assault of 24 machine guns, he just literally blew up in a bright fire.'

PO1c Maemura Tadayoshi and his crew had no hope of survival from this onslaught.

The following day another 851st Kokutai 'Mavis' fell to fighters from VF-10. Shortly after dawn, 851st Kokutai detachment commander Lt Cdr Ryu Wada was flying low over the water searching for TF 16 when *Enterprise* picked up his flying boat on radar. The FDO sent out Lt Macgregor Kilpatrick's division to intercept. Kilpatrick and Lt(jg) William Blair found Wada's 'Mavis' 30 miles northeast of *Enterprise* and the flying boat exploded under their fire.

During the course of the month both 802nd and 851st Kokutai had several encounters with USAAF B-17s. On 13 November an 802nd Kokutai 'Emily' flying from the Shortland Islands exchanged fire with a Flying Fortress, getting off one hundred and fifty 20 mm and three hundred and fifty 7.7 mm rounds without incurring any damage in return. The next day, an 851st Kokutai 'Mavis' also clashed with a B-17. Again, there was an exchange of fire without apparent effect.

One week later, on 21 November, Lt Tsuneo Hitsuji and his crew faced two separate attacks from B-17s on the same patrol south of Guadalcanal. Seeing a Flying Fortress approaching from above and to the rear, Hitsuji threw his H6K into a tight turn, the slower 'Mavis' having a smaller turning circle than the B-17. He then headed directly for the American bomber. As the two aircraft passed each other, the flying boat's tail gunner fired and hit the B-17's port inner engine, forcing the bomber to break off.

Shortly thereafter, a second Flying Fortress appeared heading straight for the 'Mavis'. Remarkably, this was B-17E 41-2433 *Miss Fit*, once again encountering an H6K while on patrol. Hitsuji recalled the combat in his book *Saigo No Hikotei* (*The Last Flying Boat*) excerpted below;

"'Okay we're ready", someone said. At an altitude of 30 metres and a speed of 150 knots, we headed towards squally skies in the direction of

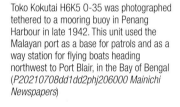

Toko Kokutai H6K5 O-35 was photographed tethered to a mooring buoy in Penang Harbour in late 1942. This unit used the Malayan port as a base for patrols and as a way station for flying boats heading northwest to Port Blair, in the Bay of Bengal (*P20210708dd1dd2phj206000 Mainichi Newspapers*)

our base. The enemy didn't start its attack immediately. It flew alongside us and passed us. I figured that it was avoiding our tail cannon. It would probably be making a frontal attack. The shoot-out was about to begin.

'"Here it comes?" someone shouted, and at the same time, the enemy's front guns and all four of our starboard machine guns started firing. As we passed each other, I could see the enemy's tail gun firing, but the tracers were way behind us. No hits on either side. We didn't change our course and headed toward the squall. The faster enemy caught up quickly and crisscrossed our path, attacking as it passed us.

'We were at very low altitude, and the sea behind us whitened with machine gun fire. As the shooting went on, this started moving closer and closer. I could not hear anything other than the roar of the machine guns and the engine noise. I couldn't keep my eyes off the enemy for a moment. The enemy made its fourth pass, and as it crossed our path, a 0.50-cal shell flew into the cockpit.

'On their sixth pass, the moment I saw their tail gun fire, there was an enormous banging noise up front. Gunner PO1 Takahashi pointed to the floor beneath the pilot's seat and I noted a big hole about 30 cm in size in the keel of our bow. I could see the waves through the hole. "If worse comes to worst we'll ram him, okay?" I patted the shoulder of the main pilot, Ens Kobayashi, with my pistol. He nodded lightly. "Okay, we're ready then". "Not yet!" I yelled, thinking that he was about to ram the B-17, but I soon realised that our co-pilot, PO1 Kira, had evaded a collision with the enemy who had come in from the side. The enemy passed about 30 metres behind us. The tail gunner poured an entire drum of 20 mm cannon shells into the B-17.'

After this final pass, the Flying Fortress broke off the combat, briefly flying alongside the 'Mavis' before disappearing into a rain squall. Hitsuji and his crew flew their badly damaged flying boat back to their Shortland Islands base. Here, it was discovered that the H6K had been holed some 93 times.

In the aftermath of these one-sided combats, the IJNAF made several modifications in the field to improve the survivability of the H6K. It covered the Type 97's fuel tanks with rubber to provide some protection, added two 20 mm cannon in the waist positions and installed 20 mm armour plating behind the pilots' seats and shields of a similar thickness for the gunners.

The final month of the year brought regular, but uneventful, patrols over the Solomons and the Central Pacific. Back in Japan, 801st Kokutai resumed operations patrolling the seas off the Japanese home islands from Yokohama. In a full year of combat, the flying boat Kokutai had lost more than 20 H6Ks and H8K1s as a direct result of enemy action, as well as an additional 35 in operational accidents. Although these aircraft could be replaced, their experienced crews could not. The fighting in the Solomons in particular had shown that the 'Mavis' could not defend itself against US Navy carrier fighters. Over the coming year, the H6K4/5 would be gradually replaced by the more capable H8K2 as Kawanishi ramped up production. However, following a hiatus in combat of nearly eight months, even the 'Emily' would face a reckoning when it encountered the F6F Hellcat.

CHAPTER FOUR

DEFENDING THE BARRIER DURING 1943

At the start of 1943 Kawanishi began building the H8K2, the Type 2 Flying Boat Model 12 being fitted with Mitsubishi Kasei Model 22 engines giving 1800 hp for take-off. It took time for the company to ramp up production, which slowed the conversion of Kokutai from the H6K4/5 to the more capable H8K2 (*2008-3-31_ image_512_01, MoF*)

A t the end of December 1942, IGHQ decided to abandon attempts to retake Guadalcanal and to withdraw Japanese forces from the island. The evacuation was completed in early February 1943. The withdrawal from Guadalcanal ceded control over the lower Solomons to the Allies, thus ending Japanese hopes of cutting off the line of communications between the USA and Australia. Heavy attrition in personnel, aircraft and ships forced the realisation that Japan had lost the initiative in the war. Going forward, it would be on the defensive.

In March 1943 the IJN issued a directive to Adm Yamamoto outlining the objectives of what was now called Third Phase operations. Its overall aim would be to destroy enemy air and naval forces advancing into designated defence zones across the Pacific.

For the flying boat Kokutai, this meant constant patrolling of their respective sectors. During the first months of the year, 851st Kokutai and 802nd Kokutai also flew offensive operations against Allied bases at Espiritu Santo and Canton Island – important way stations on the air route from the USA to Australia. The attacks on Espiritu Santo began on the night of 20 January, when a single H6K left the Shortlands and flew to the island in an attempt to target Bomber No 2 airfield. The flying boat dropped sixteen 60 kg bombs but they failed to do any damage.

A single 'Mavis' tried again on the night of 22 January, apparently dropping 14 bombs on Bomber No 1 airfield, wounding several troops but doing no damage to the facilities. Forty-eight hours later, 851st Kokutai sent another H6K to Espiritu Santo, but apparently it returned without dropping any bombs. The Kokutai tried again on the night of 26 January, but again the weather was poor and the 'Mavis' dropped its sixteen 60 kg bombs without effect.

802nd Kokutai participated in these attacks as well. On the night of 29 January, a single H8K1 left the Shortland Islands in the late afternoon, reaching Espiritu Santo sometime after midnight local time. The 'Emily' dropped twelve 60 kg bombs, with unknown results.

Three weeks later, on 21 February, an 802nd Kokutai aircraft undertook another attack when the unit received intelligence concerning the presence of Allied shipping in the harbour at Espiritu Santo. A single 'Emily' was sent to the Shortlands to work with 851st Kokutai in planning a nighttime attack. The 'Emily' arrived on the 20th and attacked Espiritu Santo the following night, dropping eight 250 kg bombs in the Segond Channel at the southern end of the island but failing to hit any allied ships.

Three months would pass before 802nd Kokutai made another attack on Espiritu Santo. On 22 May H8K1 (possibly an H8K2) arrived in the Shortland Islands from Imieji and prepared for the mission the next day. Taking off in the late afternoon, the 'Emily' arrived over Espiritu Santo around midnight and dropped eight 250 kg bombs on one of the island's airfields with undetermined results. An attempt to mount a second mission on 25 May had to be cancelled when one of the 'Emily's' generators caught fire.

Months later, on the night of 14 September, an 802nd Kokutai 'Emily' made a nighttime attack on Espiritu Santo, flying directly from Makin Island to drop sixteen 60 kg bombs in a flight lasting 13 hours.

Canton Island was also targeted during this period. Located 1660 miles from Honolulu, it was home to a newly built airfield and seaplane base. Both were attacked three times in March 1943. On the 19th, two 'Emily' flying boats took off from Imieji and hit Canton Island with thirty-one 60 kg bombs – crews involved claimed to have struck several buildings – before returning to Makin. A single 'Emily' sortied again from Makin and bombed Canton Island on the night of 22 March, dropping 14 60 kg bombs.

The following day, two 'Emilys' left Imieji for Makin to prepare for a third attack on

802nd Kokutai carried out several nocturnal bombing missions against Espiritu Santo with its H8K1s. This photograph shows an aircraft from the unit being loaded onto the seaplane carrier *Akitsushima II*. The tail code N1-13 dates the photograph as sometime in the spring of 1943 (*PG051648, Kure Maritime Museum*)

the island. Whilst taking off at the start of the mission on 24 March, one of the flying boats capsized and sank as a result of porpoising – a phenomenon that plagued H8K pilots until they were trained to cope with the problem. A seaplane tender at Makin rescued seven of the crew, but the pilot and three others were never found. The third attack was thus cancelled, although a fourth attack went out on 26 March when two 'Emilys' dropped thirty 60 kg bombs on the island, claiming hits on the runway, a hangar and the seaplane base.

OPERATIONAL DISAPPOINTMENT

As an offensive weapon, the IJNAF's flying boats did not live up to pre-war expectations. The extended fleet-versus-fleet battles the IJN had planned on, in which the flying boats would have been used to attrite the US Navy as it moved across the Pacific, never took place as envisioned. Night bombing proved far more difficult than almost all air forces expected, and even day bombing with flying boats was problematic, possibly due to the quality of the bombsights and the level of training. It is not surprising that the bombing missions flown by 'Mavis' and 'Emily' crews during 1942–43 failed to achieve much in the way of results.

During 1943, Kawanishi shifted production of flying boats from the Type 97 exclusively to the Type 2. The company stopped building the 'Mavis' in April of that year, having completed just 212 examples of all models. Production of the 'Emily' took time to build up, partly due to modifications the IJNAF instructed Kawanishi to make and partly due to shifting production to the new Konan factory 15 miles west of Osaka.

After completing 12 Type 2 Model 11 (H8K1) flying boats, Kawanishi began work on the Type 2 Model 12 (H8K2), which featured more powerful Mitsubishi Kasei Model 22 engines developing 1850 hp. Based on combat experience, the IJNAF had Kawanishi develop protection for the vulnerable fuel tanks, added armour for the pilots and gunners,

The flying boat Kokutai continued fielding H6K4/5s well into 1943 – indeed, this press photograph was taken in March 1943, and it shows groundcrew working on the engines of an H6K5 (possibly assigned to 802nd Kokutai) somewhere in the Pacific. The flying boat in the background is armed with a single 250 kg bomb attached to port wing struts (*Author's Collection*)

replaced the Type 92 7.7 mm machine gun in the bow turret with a Type 99 20 mm cannon and added more examples of the latter weapon to the two side blisters behind the wing.

Construction of the Konan factory had begun in February 1942, and it turned out its first flying boat (an H8K2) in February 1943. By August it had completed just 30 aircraft, while the Naruo factory built only three examples before stopping production of the 'Emily' in March. As a result, the three flying boat Kokutai continued flying the 'Mavis' well into 1943. 801st and 802nd

Kokutai appear to have completely re-equipped with the 'Emily' by August 1943, but 851st Kokutai was still using some H6Ks as late as March 1944. In April 1943, Sasebo Kokutai gave up its flying boats entirely, possibly to provide additional aircraft to the three dedicated frontline units.

802nd Kokutai had been ordered to withdraw from the Shortland Islands during January, moving its detachment initially to Truk and then apparently back to Imieji for patrols over the Central Pacific. The 851st Kokutai detachment withdrew during February. Early that month, on the 3rd, a B-26 Marauder from the 70th BS/38th BG had claimed a 'Mavis' shot down, although 851st Kokutai mission reports show no loss for that day – only a fleeting combat with what the 'Mavis' crew identified as a 'North American' on the 2nd, with the aircraft exchanging fire. Remarkably this would be the last Allied claim for a Japanese flying boat until August.

Having withdrawn from the Solomons, the 851st Kokutai detachment returned to the unit's original base at Toko, on Formosa, where the group spent two months undertaking patrols and flights to the Philippines and the NEI and commencing its conversion to the 'Emily'. At the end of April, 851st Kokutai transferred to Surabaya. The following month the unit set up a second base at Sibolga, on the west coast of northern Sumatra.

On 2 May, 851st Kokutai was placed under the direct command of the Southwest Fleet and instructed to patrol the Indian Ocean to the south of the NEI and the Timor Sea to northwestern Australia from Surabaya. It was to also carry out patrols over the Indian Ocean from Sibolga, searching for enemy shipping. Initially, 851st Kokutai operated both 'Mavis' and 'Emily' flying boats from Surabaya, but as the unit acquired more of the latter it gradually concentrated them at Surabaya, sending the Type 97s to Sibolga. When required, the H8K2s would fly extended patrols to reconnoitre the main harbours on Ceylon.

Between May and September the 851st Kokutai 'Emily' detachment at Surabaya flew several night reconnaissance missions over the Gulf of Carpentaria, west of the Cape York Peninsula, in Queensland, and down to Shark Bay, off the northwest coast of Western Australia, searching for shipping. The flights amply demonstrated the 'Emily's' long range.

The Surabaya H8K2s undertook more offensive missions as well. On the night of 20 March an 'Emily' flew from Ambon to the US Navy base at Exmouth, on the North Cape of Western Australia's northwest coast, dropping sixteen 60 kg bombs. That same night a second 'Emily' flew a

With its engines and cockpit protected from the salty air and oppressive heat by canvas covers, an H8K2 from 802nd Kokutai sits on its beaching gear alongside two A6M2-N 'Rufes' at Kwajalein in 1943 (*80G-214899, RG80, NARA*)

reconnaissance sortie over the Gulf of Carpentaria. On the night of the 21st, a single H8K2 again flew from Surabaya to Exmouth, where it too dropped sixteen 60 kg bombs. The ordnance dropped harmlessly into the sea, just as it had done the night before. On 22 May an 'Emily' flew from Ambon to reconnoitre the Gulf of Carpentaria.

Some weeks later, on 17 June, 851st Kokutai sent a single 'Emily' from Ambon to bomb Horn Island, the aircraft dropping sixteen 60 kg bombs without effect. The unit made a final attack on Exmouth on the night of 15 September, with a solitary 'Emily' dropping ten 60 kg bombs and seven other kinds of unidentified 'stores'. These were the final bombing missions flown by 851st Kokutai against Australia.

The unit's H8K2s were also active in carrying out reconnaissance missions over the Indian Ocean – with its long endurance, the 'Emily' could fly from Sibolga all the way to Ceylon. On the night of 16 July, in a near 16-hour mission, a single H8K2 made a night reconnaissance flight over the port of Colombo, gathering details on Allied shipping spotted in the harbour. That same night, a second 'Emily' was scheduled to carry out a similar mission over the naval base at Trincomalee, but it capsized attempting to take-off in a heavy swell and four crew were killed. Another 'Emily' tried again on the night of 18 July, and this time it reached Trincomalee.

Two months later, on the night of 19 September, a single H8K2 from 851st Kokutai returned to Colombo. Whilst there, its crew spotted transport vessels and Royal Navy warships in the harbour before returning to Sibolga to complete the 18-hour mission.

A crewman in a 35th BG B-25 captured this photograph of an 851st Kokutai 'Mavis' while strafing Rabaul's Simpson Harbour on 2 November 1943. 851st Kokutai operated the aircraft in small numbers well into 1944 (*Author's Collection*)

The RAF was not unaware of these reconnaissance missions. In September 1943 it had sent a detachment of No 176 Sqn Beaufighter VIF nightfighters to Ratmalana, in Ceylon, from Baigachi, in India, to counter these flights. The first successful interception took place on the night of 11 October, when Flt Sgt L Atkinson and his observer, Flt Sgt W Simpson, were vectored onto an 'Emily' approaching the coast of Ceylon. The chase began at 15,000 ft, descending to 6000 ft. Simpson had three fleeting contacts with the H8K on his radar but soon lost the aircraft. WO Yamazaki, at the controls of the flying boat, attempted to make good his escape, and he nearly made it, getting beyond the range of the RAF's ground control intercept radar. However, Atkinson had spotted the 'Emily' and closed in, shooting off one of the starboard engines. Another burst started a fire, and the flying boat duly crashed into the sea.

A month later, on the night of 12 November, 851st Kokutai sent out three H8K2s from Port Blair to reconnoitre Madras, on the Indian coast, Trincomalee and Colombo. The 'Emily' bound for Madras encountered a Beaufighter from the No 89 Sqn detachment tasked with protecting the city. Flt Lt R Wright and his observer, Flg Off Thompson, intercepted the flying boat and claimed to have inflicted some damage, the 'Emily' crew in turn firing fifty 20 mm rounds in their defence.

The H8K2 reconnoitring Trincomalee succeeded in noting the ships in the harbour and then returned safely home. Radio operators at Port Blair received a report from the third 'Emily' confirming that it had reached Colombo, but shortly thereafter they heard the pilot, WO Satoshi Ide, state that he was engaging an enemy aircraft. Flt Lt J G Astbury and his observer, Flg Off Ashworth, flying another No 89 Sqn Beaufighter, intercepted the 'Emily' 17 miles west of Colombo and sent it down in flames.

The F6F Hellcat's combat debut in August 1943 posed a new and dangerous threat to 'Emily' flying boat crews. During September carrier-based Hellcats claimed three H6Ks shot down over the Gilbert Islands and three more destroyed in a strafing attack on Makin Island. By war's end Hellcat pilots had claimed 38 Japanese flying boats shot down (*80G-471273, RG80, NARA*)

Lt(jg) Thaddeus Coleman from VF-6 received credit for an 'Emily' shot down on 3 September 1943, giving him his first victory of the war. Coleman became an ace flying with VF-83 from USS Essex (CV-9) during the Okinawa campaign (Essex Air Group: CVG-83, 1946)

On 8 September, five days after Lt(jg) Thaddeus Coleman's success, VF-23 pilots Lt Harold Funk and Lt(jg) Leslie Kerr Jr encountered another 'Emily' and had the presence of mind to take photographs of the flying boat as they were attacking. These provided US Navy intelligence with its first imagery of an H8K. The tail code N1-29 identifies the 'Emily' as aircraft assigned to 802nd Kokotai (80G-80446, RG80, NARA)

MORE REORGANISATION

On 1 September 1943, the IJNAF implemented another reorganisation of its land-based air units. 802nd Kokutai, which had been attached to Eleventh Koku Kantai, now came under command of 22nd Koku Sentai, which itself was assigned to the Fourth Fleet covering the Central Pacific, which also controlled 21st Koku Sentai in the Mariana Islands. By this time 802nd Kokutai had almost completely converted to the Type 2 flying boat, with four aircraft operating out of Imieji and four at Makin.

To the west, 851st Kokutai was assigned to newly formed 28th Koku Sentai, with 551st and 331st Kokutai. 28th Koku Sentai, covering mainland Southeast Asia, became part of the new Thirteenth Koku Kantai under the control of Southwestern Area Fleet, joining 23rd Koku Sentai covering the NEI. 801st Kokutai, which in May 1943 had been assigned to 27th Koku Sentai under the control of Twelfth Koku Kantai, remained within that command and continued to fly patrols out of Yokohama.

The expected American advance across the Pacific began on 31 August 1943 when a small US Navy carrier force struck Marcus Island in the combat debut of the new Essex-class fleet carriers and Independence-class light carriers. That day, 802nd Kokutai sent out several 'Emilys' on patrol towards Marcus Island in search of the American carriers, which had already retired from the area. To the south, US Army troops and engineers landed at Baker Island, east of the Gilbert Islands, to build an airfield to support the upcoming invasion of the Gilberts.

Early on the morning of 1 September, 802nd Kokutai sortied two 'Emilys' to reconnoitre Howland and Baker Islands, 600 miles away from their Gilbert Islands base on Makin Island. Lt Junsaku Kobayashi

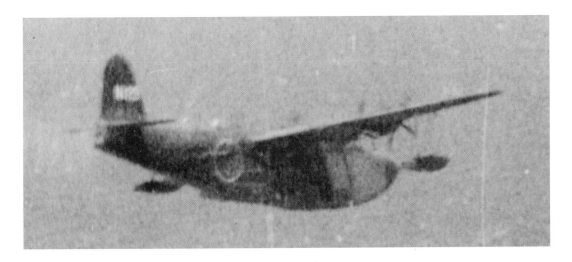

was flying near Howland Island when a division of VF-6 F6F pilots temporarily assigned to VF-23 on board USS *Princeton* (CVL-23) intercepted his flying boat. Lt(jg) Robert Loesch, the division leader, led his wingman, Ens Albert Nyquist, in a high-side, head-on run against the 'Emily', closing to within 100 yards. It is possible that their fire killed Kobayashi and his co-pilot, as the flying boat dived straight into the ocean immediately after Loesch and his wingman made their pass (the 802nd Kokutai mission report shows this loss as being on 2 September using Japan Standard Time).

Two days later, a VF-6 division had another run-in with an 'Emily'. In an extended battle, its pilot, PO Inahara Junji, made a tight turn into a cloud layer, then weaved in and out of the clouds in an attempt to escape the Hellcats. Lt(jg) Thaddeus Coleman found the 'Emily' in between the clouds and made three firing passes from the rear, noting gasoline streaming behind the outer port engine. His wingman, Ens Edward Phillipe, fired on the flying boat as it flew low over the water until it crashed.

A close-up photograph from the gun camera footage shot by one of the Hellcat pilots during a firing pass on the 802nd Kokutai H8K flown by PO Kikuchi Yoshito on 8 September 1943. The flying boat's starboard inner engine is already on fire (*80G-80448, RG80, NARA*)

Still trying to obtain intelligence on America activities on Baker Island, 802nd Kokutai lost a third H8K2 on 8 September (the mission reports identify this loss as having occurred on the 9th). Early that afternoon, VF-23 pilot Lt Harold Funk was on patrol from Baker Island with his wingman, Lt(jg) Leslie Kerr Jr, when they were vectored to intercept a 'bogey' that turned out to be an 'Emily'.

The flying boat's gunners opened fire on the attacking Hellcats as they made repeated runs at the H8K2. One of the US Navy pilots had the presence of mind to take several photographs of the 'Emily' with his gun camera, giving US Naval Intelligence its first good photos of a Type 2 flying boat.

On the initial runs, the Hellcat pilots saw hits on one of the starboard engines and gasoline streaming back from the wing. The following passes caused a fire to erupt in the forward section of the fuselage. The flying boat was soon enveloped in flames, crashing into the sea and disintegrating. With the loss of PO Kikuchi Yoshito and his crew, 802nd Kokutai was reduced in strength to just 12 crews. Five were considered to be Class A, capable of flying day or night missions, four were Class B, who could fly day missions or night missions on moonlit nights, and three were Class C, which meant they were still not fully qualified for operations.

In preparation for Operation *Galvanic* (the invasion of Tarawa), the US Navy carrier-based aircraft struck Tarawa Atoll and Makin Island on 18 September. Lt Howard Crew and his wingman, Ens Lindley Godson, from *Princeton*'s VF-23 escorted two VC-23 TBF Avengers to Makin Island, where the Hellcat pilots made eight strafing runs over the seaplane base. Two 'Emilys' from 802nd Kokutai were destroyed and a third flying boat severely damaged. The strafing and bombing attacks killed 17 members of the unit, with a further 11 missing and five severely wounded. Within the space of two weeks, 802nd Kokutai had lost more than half its strength. The unit commenced flying patrols with 'Emilys' from Makin Island again on 21 September, likely with flying boats sent from Imieji.

By then, the airfield built on Baker Island by US Army engineers had been operational for ten days, with the 15th FG's 45th FS having flown in on 11 September from Canton Island. Equipped with P-40N Warhawks, the unit immediately commenced patrols from its new home.

Just before noon on 23 October, the radar on Baker Island identified a 'bogey' south of the island. Capt Gilmer Snipes and 2Lt Russell Hendrickson were scrambled, and vectored towards the contact, they found an 'Emily' 70 miles south of Baker. This was the first Japanese aircraft the 15th FG had encountered since the 7 December 1941 attack on Wheeler Field, Hawaii. Sub Lt Mashiko Toru, pilot of the 'Emily', dived for a layer of cloud and sent out a report that he was being attacked by enemy fighters. Snipes and Hendrickson made several passes before the H8K2 entered the clouds, with the flying boat's gunners hitting Snipes' Warhawk near its engine. Unperturbed, Snipes flew through the clouds and fired on the 'Emily' when he emerged into clear skies, causing the H8K2 to explode.

802nd Kokutai appear to have lost possibly three more 'Emily' flying boats during November and December, but the mission reports for those months that could confirm the losses are missing. On 19 November, the day before the 2nd Marine Division commenced its assault on Tarawa, land- and carrier-based aircraft conducted air strikes on the atoll. Later that day, a division of four F6Fs from VF-60, flying from the escort carrier USS *Suwanee* (CVE-27), were vectored onto a 'bogey' east of Tarawa.

A strafing attack on Makin Island on 18 September 1943 cost 802nd Kokutai three H8K2s destroyed. Although heavily damaged in the attack, and the subsequent fighting on the island, this wreck provided more information on the new IJNAF flying boat for US Navy intelligence (*80G-307463, RG80, NARA*)

Lt Edward Dashiel Jr spotted a four-engined flying boat that he assumed was a 'Mavis', as up-to-date photographs of the 'Emily' had only recently begun to circulate around the fleet. Following standard US Navy doctrine, Dashiel split his division to bracket the enemy aircraft. He and his wingman came in on an overhead run, opening fire from 300 yards above the 'Emily' and raking the cockpit and engines. The outboard port engine trailed white smoke then burst into flame. As Dashiel's second section began their run, the 'Emily' entered a steep spiral that became a vertical dive, striking the water in flames. The pilots were unaware that they had shot down an H8K2, but all agreed with the identification when they saw photographs of the aircraft, likely from the earlier combat in September.

In December, US Navy patrol squadron VB-108, flying PB4Y-1 Liberators, claimed two 'Emilys' destroyed. Lt William Graham was approaching the end of his patrol sector on 2 December when his tail gunner sighted an aeroplane behind the PB4Y. Turning in pursuit, Graham caught up with an 'Emily' after a 30-minute chase. Coming in from below apparently unseen, Graham's bow and top turret gunners opened fire as the PB4Y closed to within 200 ft. They set two of the flying boat's engines on fire and knocked out the tail and dorsal turrets. However, a 20 mm shell from the waist position hit the cockpit, badly wounding Graham's feet and damaging the instrument panel. The 'Emily' fell off in a diving turn to the left, heading for a layer of cloud with its right wing on fire. Although the PB4Y crew did not see the flying boat crash, they were given credit for its destruction.

Two days later, another VB-108 PB4Y-1 attacked Jaluit Atoll, coming in over the seaplane base at Imieji and dropping two 325 lb depth charges on an 'Emily' moored there. The Liberator crew subsequently claimed the H8K2 as destroyed.

Although the flying boat units were no longer based at Rabaul, individual aircraft continued to fly in to the base to deliver personnel and supplies. In this action photograph, a bomb from a strafing USAAF B-25 falls between a 'Jake' and an 'Emily' moored in the harbour during one of the November 1943 attacks on Rabaul (*3A-31643, RG342FH, NARA*)

CHAPTER FIVE

THE BARRIER BREAKS IN 1944

After the American capture of Kwajalein, 802nd Kokutai withdrew to Saipan. From here, 801st and 802nd Kokutai flew missions evacuating personnel from bypassed bases in the Marshall Islands. This photograph of an unidentified H8K2, possibly at the seaplane base near Flores Point, was found on Saipan after its capture by US forces (*80G-169308, RG80, NARA*)

For the Japanese military, 1944 was a devastating year. When it began, the IGHQ still hoped that its forces could hold a defensive line from the Marianas down to Rabaul. However, by year-end, the Allies had captured the Marianas and much of New Guinea, landed in the Philippines, isolated Japanese bases at Rabaul and Truk and advanced into central Burma. The USAAF had begun long-range strategic bombing missions against Japan, while the US Navy's greatly expanded carrier force could roam at will across the Pacific.

As the Allied offensive progressed, there was an increasing drain on the flying boat Kokutai. During the course of the year, combat and operational losses of flying boats exceeded production at Kawanishi. While Allied air forces made claims for only five flying boats shot down between January and May 1944, from June to December, that total increased to 36.

There remained a need for long-range reconnaissance, but the capacity to undertake such missions steadily declined. At the beginning of the year, the IJNAF still had three dedicated flying boat units. By the end of 1944, just one remained.

802nd Kokutai came under increasing pressure as US forces advanced in the Central Pacific. In December 1943, the unit received instructions to withdraw its maintenance personnel from Imieji and establish a new rear area maintenance base at Saipan.

The Americans rapidly built airfields on Makin and Tarawa. During January 1944, the number of aeroplanes operating from these bases increased from 125 to 350 in preparation for the invasion of the Marshall Islands. The Japanese had expected US forces to first seize the outer Marshall Islands, but in a surprise move US Army and US Marine Corps divisions invaded Kwajalein, in the centre of the island chain, on 1 February. Aside from coming ashore on Kwajalein, troops also commenced their occupation of Roi and Namur, at the northern end of the atoll. That same day, the US Marine Corps captured Majuro. On 19 February, US Army troops landed on Eniwetok. Within days of the capture of these islands, US Marine Corps dive-bomber and fighter squadrons had moved into newly restored airfields.

The invasion of the Marshall Islands made 802nd Kokutai's long-standing base on Imieji untenable. The unit duly withdrew to Saipan with its six remaining H8K2s. 801st and 802nd Kokutai were immediately given a new mission – evacuating personnel from the now isolated island bases in the Marshalls.

Twenty-four hours after the invasion of Kwajalein, 802nd Kokutai was ordered to move to Truk. However, due to unfinished maintenance, the departure of three of the unit's flying boats was delayed until 4 February. 801st Kokutai had sent its available flying boats to Truk on the 3rd. 802nd Kokutai evacuated two warrant officers and 31 petty officers and sailors from the island of Wotje during the night of 5 February. Three 'Emilys' from 801st Kokutai proved incapable of flying at night, leaving four to carry out the mission. Two other aircraft from the unit went to Eniwetok that same night to evacuate key personnel, with three more H8K2s completing the evacuation the next night and leaving behind provisions for those who remained.

One week later, on 12 February, 801st and 802nd Kokutai flew what would prove to be the most effective IJNAF flying boat bombing mission of the war. Earlier that day, 2nd Kushu Butai had ordered the two units to carry out a night bombing mission against Roi Island.

Marine Air Group (MAG) 31 had arrived on Roi on 7 February, five days after the island's capture, to begin preparing the airfield for fighter and dive-bomber squadrons. That night, 801st and 802nd Kokutai each sent out three H8K2s from Truk. The 'Emilys' arrived over Roi at around 0300 hrs local time, dropping large amounts of 'window' (aluminium strips later known as 'chaff') to confuse radar on the island. The flying boats dropped 250 kg bombs and light incendiaries. One of the first bombs hit the island's ammunition dump, and the resulting explosion destroyed 80 per cent of the supplies on the island and 20 per cent of the construction equipment. The US Marine Corps had 26 personnel killed and 130 wounded, while the two US Navy construction battalions (Seabees) on the island suffered 157 casualties. All the flying boats returned safely to Truk.

801st Kokutai then went back to flying regular patrols out of Yokohama, but it was also instructed to use a greater number of its H8K2s to transport aviation equipment from Japan to Saipan. In early March 801st Kokutai had four Type 97s (two H6K4s and two H6K5s), ten H8K2s

On 31 March 1944, Adm Mineichi Koga, commander of the Combined Fleet, lost his life in the crash of an 851st Kokutai H8K2 that ran into bad weather flying from Palau to Davao (*NH 63695, NHHC*)

and one H6K2-L transport available. 802nd Kokutai had possibly as many as six H8K2s at Saipan. Towards the end of March, the unit was ordered to transfer its aircraft to Truk, where, on 25 March, 802nd Kokutai was disbanded and its flying boats incorporated into the reconnaissance unit of the Fourteenth Koku Kantai. IJNAF Koku Kantai held certain types of aircraft, including flying boats, in a headquarters unit to transport senior officers and equipment and apparently formed some of these aircraft into a separate reconnaissance unit.

This left the IJNAF with 801st Kokutai, assigned to 27th Koku Sentai with Twelfth Koku Kantai under the Northeastern Area Fleet, and 851st Kokutai, still assigned to 23rd Koku Sentai with Thirteenth Koku Kantai under the Southwest Area Fleet. An 802nd Kokutai crew would, however, participate in one more mission with the H8K2 flying boat. It ended in disaster.

At the end of March the US Navy's Fast Carrier Task Force, now TF 58, struck IJN bases and shipping at Palau. Adm Mineichi Koga, commander of the Combined Fleet, decided to move his headquarters from Palau to Saipan via Davao. On 30 March Adm Koga ordered 851st Kokutai to have three flying boats standing by at Davao for him and his staff. Two of the H8K2s then flew to Palau, where a third joined them for the mission.

The first 851st Kokutai 'Emily' left Palau at 2230 hrs local time, carrying Koga and seven of his staff, with Lt Masatada Namba as his pilot. The second 'Emily', with Sub Lt Matsutaro Okamura from 802nd Kokutai at the controls and carrying Koga's chief of staff, Vice Adm Fukudome Shigeru, and ten staff members, left a little later. A third H8K2, flown by Sub Lt Toshikane Ando from 851st Kokutai and carrying the Combined Fleet Headquarters cryptographers, departed at 0456 hrs on 31 March.

By 0300 hrs at Davao – the estimated time of arrival of the first and second flying boats – neither aircraft had landed or could be contacted on radio. Apparently, both had run into a typhoon en route to Davao. Koga's aircraft had crashed, killing all on board. Later that afternoon (31 March), it was learned that the second 'Emily' had force-landed near Cebu Island and Vice Adm Fukudome had been captured by Philippine guerillas. The IJA in Cebu immediately began an intensive and brutal search for Fukudome, who was finally released on 11 April. He had been carrying battle plans for Operation *Z*, detailing how the Combined Fleet would oppose an Allied assault on Japan's inner defensive barrier from the Marianas to western New Guinea. These plans apparently found their way to Allied Intelligence.

Earlier in March, both 801st and 802nd Kokutai had undertaken eight flights into Rabaul from Truk. 801st Kokutai and, later, 851st Kokutai completed four more flights in April and four in early May. Each H8K2 could carry 35 personnel, and over the course of these flights the two units evacuated more than 500 personnel to Truk and then on to Saipan. More flights took place on 7 and 10 June, when flying boats shuttled between Saipan and Buin, on Bougainville, via Truk, delivering medical supplies and evacuating personnel. These flights did not resume until March 1945.

ASW KOKUTAI

In early 1944, a new unit began operating flying boats. On 18 December 1943, the IJNAF activated 901st Kokutai at Tateyama, in Japan, as the first air unit dedicated to convoy escort and ASW – two areas where the IJNAF had been astonishingly lax. As an IJN officer commented after the war, 'convoy escort and ASW patrols are monotonous and defensive – far from the IJN's fixation with offensive naval warfare'. But a sharp increase in shipping losses in the autumn of 1943 made the IJN realise that the effectiveness of the torpedoes being fired by US Navy submarines had improved dramatically.

In November 1943, the IJN established the Grand Escort Command Headquarters (GEHQ) to supervise protection for Japanese shipping, including providing unified control over routing convoys and ASW. When activated, 901st Kokutai was assigned to GEHQ.

At the start, the unit had little to build on. No IJNAF airmen had experience in ASW and there was no mission doctrine. 901st Kokutai personnel effectively had to learn by doing. From activation, the unit contained a mix of aircraft. It commenced operations in January 1944 with 12 G3M 'Nell' bombers, based in Japan, and three H6K 'Mavis' flying boats operating out of Toko, at the southern tip of Formosa. 901st Kokutai added more flying boats as they became available. In February, the unit sent several H6Ks to bases in Japan, six more to Toko for patrolling over the South China Sea and two to Saipan to cover convoys sailing there from Japan via Iwo Jima.

With the main flying boat units converting to the H8K2 'Emily', more of the older H6Ks became available, and by March 1944 901st Kokutai had no fewer than 32 'Mavis' flying boats on strength, as well as 48 'Nells'. The detachment on Saipan grew to six H6Ks, and in April four flying boats were sent to Saigon for operations off Indochina. In June 901st Kokutai began receiving H8K2s, and it started using these on patrols from Toko and Davao alongside the H6Ks.

In the second half of the year the IJNAF began equipping 901st Kokutai H6K4s with airborne search radar and a Magnetic Airborne Detection (MAD) device to better search for American submarines – sometimes both devices were installed on the same aircraft. On daylight patrols, when submarines tended to remain submerged, a 'Mavis' would use the MAD. At night, with vessels operating on the surface under the cover of darkness, crews would revert to search radar to detect submarines. If a 'Mavis' located a submarine, it would have to radio for other aircraft to attack for the flying boat lacked bombs or depth charges.

During March 1944, the flying boats operating out of Toko had several encounters with Fourteenth Air Force B-24s from the 308th BG as the USAAF bombers conducted sweeps over the South China Sea. On 19 March, 1Lt Glenn McConnell from the group's 373rd BS was flying a radar-equipped B-24D on a sea search mission when his crew spotted what they initially thought was another B-24 ahead of them. Recognising the aeroplane as a 'Mavis', McConnell went in to attack. His gunners set its No 3 engine on fire and the Japanese pilot pulled up into a cloud layer, McConnell losing contact. The pilot of the 'Mavis' radioed that he had engaged a B-24 in combat, and his right engine was now on fire. That was the last the Toko base heard from the crew.

The H6K5 continued to be used until the end of the war, many with Koku Kantai and Koku Sentai headquarters and transport units. A PB4Y-1 from VB-109 caught this H6K5 of an unknown unit on 7 May 1944. Once the wing tanks had caught fire, a 'Mavis' was effectively doomed (*80G-227384, RG80, NARA*)

To his surprise, McConnell ran into the same 'Mavis' 45 minutes later. Again, his crew opened fire, as did the gunners in the 'Mavis' – bullets hit the B-24's cockpit, wounding McConnell and his flight engineer and knocking out several instruments. However, the gunners in the Liberator started another fire between the Nos 3 and 4 engines, causing the flying boat's wing to break off and the aircraft to crash into the sea.

On 27 March single B-24s from the 308th BG's 374th and 425th BSs combined to claim another 'Mavis', although 901st Kokutai mission reports do not record this loss.

In the western Pacific the flying boat units had suffered few losses up to mid-1944. Several H6Ks and H8K2s had fallen to the guns of patrolling PB4Y-1 Liberators but none to US Navy carrier fighters. June, however, would see the highest number of IJNAF flying boats lost in combat during World War 2. During the attacks on the Marianas between 11 and 22 June, US Navy Hellcats would claim 12 'Emily' and 'Mavis' flying boats shot down and six destroyed at the Tanapag seaplane base on Saipan.

Following Adm Koga's death and the exposure of Operation *Z* to the Allies, the IJN staff in Tokyo prepared a new plan, Operation *A-GO*, which would mobilise the Combined Fleet to defend the inner barrier. Adm Soemu Toyoda, who replaced Koga as commander of the Combined Fleet, prepared for a decisive battle against the US Navy when it could be definitively located.

American landings on Biak, at the western end of New Guinea, on 27 May distracted Japanese attention from the impending assault on the Marianas. By then, 851st Kokutai had moved its eight 'Emilys' to Davao to carry out evacuation and transport missions. The unit received orders to stay there and conduct patrols over the southwestern areas in search of US Navy vessels. 801st Kokutai remained at Yokohama patrolling sectors to the east and southeast of Japan. 5th Kushu Butai, controlling 61st and 62nd Koku Sentai in the Marianas, did not have any flying boats attached. It appears that the reconnaissance units from First and Eleventh Koku Kantai stationed several flying boats at Saipan.

The worst day for flying boat losses was 11 June, which was also the date that TF 58's carriers commenced strikes on the Marianas. Early that morning, a division of Hellcats from VF-1 flying off USS *Yorktown* (CV-10) were on CAP 44 miles from the Task Force when they were vectored onto an incoming 'bogey'. The division identified the aircraft as an 'Emily' flying at 2000 ft. Seeing the Hellcats, the pilot of the H8K2 dived for the water below while the turret gunner fired 20 mm cannon rounds at the pursuers. The four Hellcats made repeated passes from starboard and port sides, hitting the cockpit area and setting the starboard engines on fire.

The 'Emily' entered a gentle turn to starboard until the starboard wing hit the water and the flying boat flipped over onto its back and crashed.

A short time later, a division from VF-2 off USS *Hornet* (CV-12) were flying CAP over a picket destroyer 50 miles from the Task Force. In the space of an hour, the division encountered two 'Emilys' and a 'Betty' bomber searching for the task force and shot down all three, Lt Cdr Leroy Harris claiming the first flying boat and Lt(jg) Franklin Gabriel the second.

Another division from VF-1 then encountered an 'Emily' while on CAP after also receiving a vector to intercept a 'bogey'. After taking charge of his division when his leader's radio failed, Lt(jg) Arthur Payton Jr sighted the 'Emily' flying 4000 ft below him at 9000 ft. Payton promptly made a high-side run on the H8K2, hitting its starboard side and the starboard inner engine. Diving for the sea and firing at the attacking Hellcats as the other members of the division made repeated runs on the flying boat, the 'Emily' finally crashed into the water. Flying over the debris, one of the Hellcat pilots saw an empty life raft and a crewman in a life jacket. Astonishingly, two members of the crew had survived the crash. A destroyer on picket duty picked them up and also found sacks of mail, indicating that the flying boat, probably from either 801st or 851st Kokutai, had been taking personnel from Buin to Saipan when it unknowingly stumbled into the division of Hellcats.

Around midday, TF 58 launched 213 Hellcats, ten SB2C Helldivers and an undisclosed number of TBM Avengers for strikes against Japanese airfields and harbours on Saipan, Guam and Tinian. Task Group (TG) 58.4 sent 39 Hellcats from VF-15, VF-25 and VF-32 and two dive-bombers to attack the Japanese seaplane base at Flores Point, near Tanapag Harbor on Saipan. The Hellcats from VF-25 appear to have arrived in the area first, and seeing no aircraft in the air, went down to strafe flying boats spotted on the water.

After completing their attack, the pilots claimed one 'Mavis' destroyed on the water and three 'Emilys' damaged on the water and on the seaplane ramp. Following several strafing runs, VF-25 CO Lt Cdr Gaylord Brown flew down the west coast of Saipan in search of targets, before returning to the seaplane base to make two runs on an 'Emily' moored off Flores Point. Leaving it burning fiercely, Brown claimed the aircraft destroyed. Lt(jg) Relly Raffman and his wingman were flying northwest of the seaplane base, chasing a Japanese fighter, when they saw an 'Emily' approaching Saipan from the northeast. Turning their attention to the flying boat, they made three or four runs on the 'Emily' that set its engines on fire and sent the aircraft crashing into the water.

VF-15 and VF-32 struck the seaplane base shortly thereafter. Seven Hellcats from VF-15 armed with 350 lb depth charges began the attack, approaching in line abreast formation and strafing as they released their bombs. The remaining eight F6Fs from the unit followed in their wake, also strafing in line abreast formation. Cdr Charles Brewer, CO of VF-15,

The American invasion of the Marianas was costly to the IJANF's flying boat units. During the 11 June 1944 attack on Saipan, US Navy fighters and bombers claimed seven 'Emilys' and a 'Mavis' shot down and five 'Emilys' and a 'Mavis' destroyed at the seaplane base at Flores Point, shown here under attack that morning (*80G-384164, RG80, NARA*)

One of the H8K2 flying boats destroyed at the seaplane base at Flores Point. The tail code of 1-006 may indicate that the flying boat was assigned to 801st Kokutai, which routinely flew aircraft to Saipan delivering medical supplies and evacuating personnel back to Japan (*2009-08-13A_image_001_01, MoF*)

dropped his depth charge in the centre of two 'Emilys' and a 'Jake' (Aichi E13A floatplane), destroying all three. The strafing and bombing by VF-15 and VF-32 destroyed five 'Emilys' and one 'Mavis' on the seaplane ramp, and possibly additional flying boats on the water – the volume in the *Senshi Sosho* (*War History*) series on the Marianas battle states that the IJNAF lost six large flying boats in this attack.

Coming off his strafing run, Cdr Brewer and his wingman, Ens Richard Fowler, were flying northwest of Marpi Point, at the northern tip of Saipan, when they saw an 'Emily' approaching. They duly attacked the flying boat in conjunction with other Hellcats. This is likely to have been the same flying boat claimed by VF-25.

Later that afternoon, Lt William Maxwell of VF-51, embarked in USS *San Jacinto* (CVL-30), claimed an 'Emily' shot down east of Tinian. At some point during the day a fortunate 901st Kokutai flying boat on patrol received a hurried call to return to Chichi Jima, thus avoiding the disaster taking place on Saipan.

The attrition of flying boats around the Marianas continued. On 16 June two VF-32 pilots claimed an 'Emily' shot down after a 20-minute chase and ten-minute battle. The Hellcat pilots, Lt William Hudspeth and Lt(jg) Lloyd McEachern, fired 3350 rounds of 0.50-cal ammunition in repeated passes, and they were impressed with the 'Emily's' ability to absorb their fire before crashing.

On the first day (19 June) of the Battle of the Philippine Sea, a PB4Y-1 from VB-101 caught an 'Emily', possibly from 801st Kokutai, south of Guam and shot it down. That same day, the IJNAF had three flying boats available at Truk and six with 851st Kokutai at Davao. To maintain patrol coverage, 851st Kokutai was ordered to send four H8K2s to Palau. On 22 June carrier fighters from VF-8, embarked in USS *Bunker Hill* (CV-17), and VF-14, embarked in USS *Wasp* (CV-18), claimed two 'Emilys' shot down west of the Marianas.

Following the Battle of the Philippine Sea, 801st and 851st Kokutai continued to fly daily patrols over their assigned sectors. In July, 801st Kokutai, which remained at Yokohama with ten H8K2s, was transferred from 27th Koku Sentai to Third Koku Kantai, which did not result in any change in its mission. 851st Kokutai had several 'Emilys' undertake sorties

from Davao and Palau, with some flying boats continuing to operate out of Port Blair and Singapore. 851st Kokutai lost an H8K2 on 2 July to a patrolling PB4Y-1 from VB-115, the crew of the latter taking some dramatic close-up photographs of the hapless flying boat before it was shot down.

US Navy carrier fighters also continued to take a toll of 'Emilys' searching for American task forces. TF 58 sent TGs 58.1 and 58.2 to attack Japanese bases at Iwo Jima and Chichi Jima on 3–4 July, and on the 3rd VF-2 claimed another 'Emily' snooper shot down. The unit claimed two more on a return visit to the Bonin Islands on 5 August, with one of the flying boats being shot down just 225 miles from Tokyo – VF-8 added a third 'Emily' that same day.

The continuing attrition of flying boats and the change in Japan's strategic situation following the fall of the Marianas led the IJNAF to disband 851st Kokutai on 20 September. At the beginning of that month, the unit had just four operational H8K2s and 11 crews. The IJNAF apparently decided that at this stage of the war floatplanes like the E13A 'Jake', which had a range of 1298 miles, could take over some of the patrol missions previously assigned to the flying boats. More critically, the IJNAF needed additional personnel to mount a defence against the next American advance, which was likely to fall on the Philippines or Okinawa. 851st Kokutai transferred its remaining H8K2s to 801st Kokutai.

By now it was obvious that the 'Emily', despite its heavy armament and protected fuel tanks, had little chance on daylight missions against US Navy carrier fighters backed by excellent radar and fighter direction. The IJNAF had equipped the latest production versions of the H8K2 with airborne search radar, making them capable of flying search missions by night, but soon even the cover of darkness would prove no safeguard against a new threat – US Navy carrier-based nightfighters.

With the loss of the Marianas, IGHQ set out a new policy for the defence of Japan called Operation *Sho* (*Victory*). *Sho-Ichi-Go* (*Victory No 1*) covered the defence of the Philippines, *Sho-Ni-Go* (*Victory No 2*) the defence of Formosa and the Ryukyu Islands, *Sho-San-Go* (Victory No 3) the defence of the Japanese homeland and *Sho-Yon-Go* (Victory No 4) the defence of Hokkaido and the Kuriles. To defend these territories,

This remarkably close photograph of an H8K2 from 851st Kokutai, taken on 2 July 1944 from an attacking PB4Y-1 of VB-115, shows the 'Emily's' armament of dorsal, waist and rear turret-mounted Type 99 20 mm cannon. The weapon housed in the dorsal turret appears to be pointing away from the PB4Y-1, indicating that the Liberator gunners may have knocked it out of action (*80G-241258, RG80, NARA*)

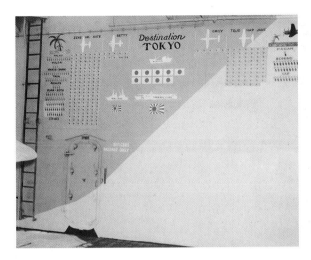

Over the summer of 1944 the flying boat Kokutai suffered heavily from US Navy fighter attacks on the Marianas and, later, on the Bonin Islands. This photograph shows the scoreboard applied to *Hornet*'s island towards the end of August, listing VF-2's claims for five 'Emilys' (80G-244910, RG80, NARA)

the IJNAF reorganised its land-based air power, creating Second Koku Kantai to defend Formosa and the Ryukyus, with First Koku Kantai defending the Philippines and Third Koku Kantai defending the Japanese homeland. Composed of many inexperienced pilots, the three Koku Kantai conducted intensive training in preparation for Operation *Sho*.

Following the fall of the Marianas, American objectives shifted to the Philippines, with a projected landing on Leyte advanced to 20 October. To reduce Japanese air defences prior to the Leyte invasion, Adm William Halsey took TF 38 (TF 58 became TF 38 when Halsey was commander of the Third Fleet) to strike at the Second Koku Kantai airfields on Okinawa and Formosa. TF 38 surprised the Japanese with its strike against Okinawa on 10 October. That morning, the commander of the Combined Fleet gave the order to initiate the *Sho-Ni-Go* for the defence of Formosa. Adm Shigeru Fukudome immediately ordered 801st Kokutai to send ten flying boats to operate from the base at Toko.

801st Kokutai began flying night searches with radar-equipped H8K2s, while 901st Kokutai used its H6Ks that also featured airborne search radar. On the night of 10 October, flying boats from both units detected two enemy task forces sailing east of Formosa. 901st Kokutai sent out three H6Ks early the following morning, and each flying boat soon located enemy forces and radioed their findings back to Toko. At 0350 hrs local time, Toko ordered the three flying boats to leave their search areas immediately and retreat to Hong Kong after refuelling at Mako due to likely impending air attacks on Formosa.

The *Senshi Sosho* states that American carrier aircraft strafed two of these flying boats while they were at Mako and sank both of them. However, TG 38 reported that 16 Hellcats from VF-11 off *Hornet* attacked the Toko seaplane base on 12 October and destroyed three 'Mavis' flying boats found in the harbour with gun fire and eight five-inch rockets. VF-11 made another attack on Toko the next day, strafing two newly arrived Mavis flying boats. Despite numerous passes, the Hellcat pilots failed to set them on fire. Another F6F division from an unknown squadron then attacked, and the H6K4s were destroyed.

During the early morning hours of 13 October, Hellcat pilots from VF(N)-41 flying off USS *Independence* (CVL-22) – a dedicated nightfighter carrier – claimed three 'Emilys' shot down near the Toko seaplane base.

That evening, the squadron sent off four teams of TBM-1 Avengers and F6F-5N Hellcats to bomb airfields in southwestern Formosa. Ens Jack Berkheimer became separated from his TBM teammate in bad weather south of Toko, but flying near the base he saw three four-engined flying boats in the harbour. He was about to make a strafing run when wing lights on an aeroplane passed on his port side. Berkheimer identified this as an 'Emily', and turned in pursuit, opening fire from the 'five o'clock' position. He set the two inboard engines alight, and a subsequent burst also started

a fire in the hull, sending the 'Emily' down to crash into the sea near the seaplane base. Berkheimer then made a bombing and strafing run on Toko.

Heading north up the west coast of Formosa towards Ryukyu Island, Berkheimer saw another set of wing lights on a second 'Emily'. Closing in from directly behind, but unseen, he opened fire and set the port engines alight, before starting another fire in the hull with his8 next burst. Soon, the 'Emily' was enveloped in flames and crashed.

Squadronmate Ens Robert Klock also found an 'Emily' flying in the same area, having seen a mass of flames from one of Berkheimer's victims. He, too, approached from the 'six o'clock' position and fired into the flying boat's engines, watching the 'Emily' spiral down into the sea.

On 15 October, Lt William Henry, also from VF(N)-41, was flying a night CAP when he was vectored onto a 'bogey' 25 miles from *Independence*. After a difficult pursuit, he closed on his target and opened fire. His first burst missed, but his second hit the inboard port engine and his third the inboard starboard engine. With fires in both engines, the enemy aircraft, which he had identified as an 'Emily', made an uncontrolled dive to the right and crashed into the water.

Nine days later, Ens Jack Berkheimer again claimed two flying boats while performing a night CAP on a dark, moonless evening over TF 38. Having downed an 'Emily', he was then vectored onto another 'bogey' that turned out to be a 'Mavis'. Its pilot knew he was under attack, resorting to continuous manoeuvres in the hope of evading Berkheimer, who persisted in his pursuit and eventually hit the flying boat's inboard engines, followed by the starboard outer engine. The wing of the H6K eventually caught fire and the flying boat crashed.

The F6F-5N nightfighter proved to be a new menace for IJNAF flying boats that had switched to flying night searches when losses by day proved prohibitive. Here, an F6F-5N from VF(N)-41 prepares to take off from *Independence* on 10 October 1944. In the final months of that year the unit would claim nine 'Emily' and 'Mavis' flying boats shot down at night (*80G-290024, RG80, NARA*)

The depredations of the US Navy nightfighters continued on 24 October when Cdr James Gray Jr, a nightfighter pilot who had just taken command of VF-20 embarked in *Enterprise*, claimed a 'Mavis'. This appears to have been a 901st Kokutai H6K sent out from Toko to search for the American carriers. Lt Shigemi Yamanouchi radioed that he had detected an enemy force east of Luzon, but his aeroplane never returned. Another VF(N)-41 pilot claimed a second 'Mavis' three days later. Lt Henry made the final nightfighter claims of 1944 when he shot down 'Emilys' on 19 November and 14 December.

In three months, US Navy nightfighters had claimed ten 'Mavis' and 'Emily' flying boats shot down. PB4Y squadrons claimed an additional five flying boats downed on their patrols. The IJNAF reported the loss of eight flying boats in October, nine in November and three in December, adding to 34 destroyed in action between January and September. In addition, the units suffered the same number of flying boats lost for operational reasons.

A lesser known aspect of IJNAF flying boat operations is how the aircraft undertook transport flights. Kawanishi built 20 H6K4-L transports and converted two more from H6K airframes. In 1943, the company began building a transport version of the H8K2 as the H8K2-L Seiku (Clear Sky), completing 36 by 1945. The IJN's Area Fleets and Air Fleets had attached Transport Aircraft Units equipped with four to six aircraft, some of which were H6K4-L or later H8K2-L flying boats.

The IJNAF maintained three full transport Kokutai, namely 1001st, 1081st and 1021st Kokutai. 1001st and 1081st Kokutai were subordinated to the Combined Fleet, with 1021st Kokutai, activated at the start of 1944, assigned to First Koku Kantai as part of 61st Koku Sentai. For much of 1944, 1021st Kokutai had detachments in Japan, Peleliu, Yap, Davao and at Clark Field, near Manila. These flying boats carried personnel and equipment over the IJN's transport routes, ranging from Paramushiro in the far north to Batavia in the southwest and to the islands in the Central Pacific for as long as they remained under Japanese control.

The IJNAF instructed Kawanishi to develop a transport version of the H8K2 as the H8K2-L. The company modified the 13-Shi prototype into a transport, as this photograph appears to show. The aeroplane was later assigned to Yokosuka Kokutai, where it served alongside other H8K2-L transports. The unit named the aircraft *Shikishima* (*Scattered Islands*) apparently after an IJN battleship that fought in the famous naval battle of Tsushima in 1905 (2008-3-31_image_510_01, Peter M Bowers Collection, MoF)

CHAPTER SIX

THE FINAL MONTHS

By early 1945 Japan's situation had become desperate. The attempt to defeat the Americans in the Philippines had failed, resulting in heavy losses, even with the advent of the kamikaze. The home islands were under attack from B-29s in the Marianas, and it seemed only a matter of time before American forces would be on Japan's doorstep. The need for long-range flying boats was diminishing just as the IJNAF was desperate for fighter aircraft that could stand a chance against the latest US Navy and USAAF fighters and bombers.

In March 1945 the IJNAF ordered Kawanishi to stop production of the H8K2 and concentrate instead on the N1K2-J Shiden-Kai ('George') fighter and the twin-engined Yokosuka P1Y2 Ginga ('Frances') medium bomber that it had instructed the company to build. Kawanishi's Konan factory built nine H8K2s between January and April 1945.

901st Kokutai continued flying convoy escort and ASW missions, although the loss of aircraft equipped with airborne search radar and MAD devices in the October–November 1944 battles had been severe. Nevertheless, by January 1945 it still had nearly 200 aircraft of different types, including 12 flying boats, on strength. However, a change in shipping routes meant that 901st Kokutai no longer needed long-range flying boats. Marauding US Navy submarines and patrol aircraft based in the Philippines had made the South China Sea too dangerous for large convoys. Shipping now had to hug the shores up the China coast to Korea

Two H8K2-L transports that flew with Yokosuka Kokutai sit on their beaching gear at Yokosuka air base shortly after war's end. Behind them is what appears to be an Aichi E16A1 Zuiun, codenamed 'Paul' by the Allies. Less than 260 examples of this late-war reconnaissance floatplane were built, and Yokosuka Kokutai was one of only three units to fly them operationally (*GAF_image_086_01, MoF*)

801st Kokutai provided pathfinder and weather reconnaissance flying boats to Azusa Tokubetsu Kogekitai for Operation *Tan No 2* – the attack on the US Navy anchorage at Ulithi Atoll – on 11 March 1945. Here, Azusa aircrew march past an H8K2 in the direction of their P1Y1 'Frances' bombers (*P20210805dd1dd1phj704000, Mainichi Newspapers*)

and on to the home islands. Single-engined floatplanes and land-based attack bombers had more than enough range to escort convoys. By May 1945 901st Kokutai was no longer operating flying boats.

801st Kokutai continued as a dedicated flying boat unit until April 1945. It appears to have flown regular patrol missions with five H8K2s from Kagoshima, on the island of Kyushu, and three from the seaplane base at Takuma, near Mitoyo on the island of Shikoku in the Inland Sea.

In late February 1945 the IJNAF assigned the three H8K2s at Takuma to assist in an attack on the US Navy anchorage at Ulithi Atoll, in the Caroline Islands, codenamed Operation *Tan No 2*. The plan called for 24 P1Y1 'Frances' medium bombers, drawn from 762nd Kokutai and formed into Azusa Tokubetsu Kogekitai (Special Attack Unit), to fly to Ulithi and crash into US Navy aircraft carriers moored in the anchorage. Five H8K2s from 801st Kokutai were made available to provide weather reconnaissance and act as pathfinders leading the P1Y1s towards Ulithi.

Following delays, the mission finally commenced on 11 March when an 'Emily' set out on a weather reconnaissance from Kagoshima two hours before Azusa Tokubetsu Kogekitai departed Kanoya at 0900 hrs local time. Two more H8K2s led the 'Frances' formation to the small island of Minami-Daito Jima, east of Okinawa. En route, six of the P1Y1s had to return to Kanoya with engine trouble and one of the H8K2 pathfinders disappeared, most likely having fallen victim to a PB4Y-2 from VPB-118 flown by Lt Norman Keiser. Upon reaching Minami-Daito Jima, the surviving H8K2 turned back and the remaining P1Y1s pressed on. Only two reached Ulithi, where one crashed into USS *Randolph* (CV-15) and inflicted considerable damage on the stern of the aircraft carrier.

During March and early April 801st Kokutai lost four 'Emilys' to US Navy carrier aircraft, including one improbably shot down at night by a TBM Avenger. The US Navy's Fast Carrier Task Force, now back as TF 58 under Adm Raymond Spruance, launched strikes against Japanese airfields on Kyushu and Shikoku on 18–19 March as a prelude to the invasion of Okinawa, codenamed Operation *Iceberg*.

On one of the early morning strikes on the 18th, a division of Hellcats from VF-30, embarked in USS *Belleau Wood* (CVL-24), encountered an 801st Kokutai 'Emily'. Ens Carl Foster made two flat-side runs on it, setting an engine on fire and triggering a huge explosion aft of the cockpit that sent the flying boat down out of control.

Early the next morning, VF(N)-90 launched five TBM-3D Avengers, equipped with APS-3 airborne search radar, from *Independence* to search for shipping in the Inland Sea. Lt Charles Henderson, having attacked two destroyer escorts in the Bungo Channel between Kyushu and Shikoku, was continuing his patrol when a 'bogey' appeared above him on the Avenger's search radar. Henderson climbed to 8500 ft, and through careful coordination between himself and his radar operator, he intercepted an 'Emily' probably returning from a mission searching for TF 58.

Henderson closed on the flying boat from astern, following the 'Emily's' tail light. He fired several bursts from his fixed 0.50-cal machine guns into the aircraft's engines, lowering the Avenger's landing gear to avoid overshooting the H8K2 as it spiralled down towards the sea. The flying boat pulled out at 30 ft, at which point a final burst from Henderson into the engines sent it down to explode as it hit the water.

801st Kokutai lost two more H8K2s over Okinawa, one on 27 March and another on 12 April.

On 25 April the IJNAF's Fifth Koku Kantai, established two months earlier, ordered that all remaining flying boat Kokutai and their aircraft be combined into one unit, Takuma Kokutai. Activated in June 1943, Takuma Kokutai had provided training for seaplane and flying boat crews until reorganised as a combat Kokutai on 20 April 1945. 801st and 901st Kokutai duly transferred their few remaining operational H6K and H8K2 flying boats to Takuma Kokutai. 801st Kokutai re-equipped with G4M 'Betty' bombers.

Takuma Kokutai was composed of a flying boat unit and a Tokubetsu Kogekitai of E13A 'Jakes'. As of 27 April, Takuma Kokutai had five H8K2s and one H6K operational and six under repair. Its 'Emilys' undertook night reconnaissance missions searching for American task forces around Okinawa that could then be targeted by Tokubetsu Kogekitai (kamikaze) units under Fifth Koku Kantai control. The solitary H6K flew missions to Amami Gunto, an island northeast of Okinawa, to pick up stranded aircrew who had made it back to the island from attacks around Okinawa.

It appears that the IJNAF had contemplated another attack on Ulithi Atoll in Operation *Tan No 3*, as Takuma Kokutai sent an H8K2 carrying maintenance personnel for the P1Y1 from Yokohama to Truk during the night of 29 April. This aircraft appears to have fallen victim to a P-47N from the 73rd FS the following day, the Thunderbolt-equipped unit having moved to Ie Shima, on Okinawa, with the 318th FG just hours earlier.

Takuma Kokutai continued flying night reconnaissance missions during May and June, heading out to a point 400 miles off the shores of Japan. On 1 June the unit had four H8K2s and one H6K operational. A month later, there were six H8K2s available. In early July, Takuma Kokutai received an urgent request to send flying boats to Nanao, on Japan's west coast, and two or three H8K2s operated from

This burning 'Mavis' was the penultimate US Navy victory over an IJNAF flying boat. Lt Cdr Allen Waggoner and his crew from Liberator-equipped VPB-116 claimed the aircraft shot down south of Shizuoka on 9 May 1945. The next day two PB2Y-5 Coronado flying boats from VPB-13 combined to shoot down a 'Mavis' west of Nagasaki (*80G-490083, RG80, NARA*)

In the final months of the war there were few 'Emilys' that were still operational. This photograph of a beached H8K2-L likely from 1021st Kokutai, taken after VJ Day, is representative of the state of the remaining IJNAF flying boats by war's end (*NH 95042, NHHC*)

The IJNAF left aircraft across the breadth of what had been the Greater East Asia Co-Prosperity Sphere. Here, RAF Servicing Commandos work on the engines of an H6K4-L transport at the IJN base at Surabaya, on the island of Java in the NEI. The flying boat has both surrender markings and Indonesian colours applied. The original caption states that the airmen were preparing the flying boat for an air test, which, if completed, would have been the last time an H6K took to the skies (*CF. 1074, Imperial War Museum*)

the port later in the month, likely flying patrols over the Sea of Japan. July also brought more night reconnaissance missions searching for US Navy task forces, with mixed results, as enemy vessels were rarely found.

Towards the end of July, Takuma Kokutai used two elderly H6Ks to evacuate 20 IJNAF aircrew and 50 base personnel from Amami Gunto back to Kitajima air base on Shikoku. By 31 July, Takuma Kokutai appears to have had no flying boats operational at its main base, and just three airworthy 'Emilys' at Nanao. Several H8K2s and H6Ks were in various states of repair. Few missions were likely to have been flown before war's end.

A solitary H8K2 survived the conflict. The US Navy acquired one of the Takuma Kokutai 'Emilys' and shipped it back to Naval Air Station (NAS) Patuxent River, Maryland, to test the H8K2's hydrodynamic characteristics. On arrival at Patuxent River, the 'Emily's' engines went through extensive reconditioning. The US Navy conducted taxiing tests until the failure of two engines forced the trials to be curtailed. US Navy test pilots concluded that the 'Emily's' hydrodynamic characteristics were inferior to comparable American flying boats, specifically the XPB2Y-1, PB2Y-5, XPBS-1 and XPBB-1. Where the 'Emily' did prove superior was in its spray characteristics. The longitudinal strips attached to the lower hull beneath the cockpit were effective in preventing spray from the bow wave created on take-off from reaching the propellers.

APPENDICES

COLOUR PLATES COMMENTARY

1
F.5 S-41, Sasebo Kaigun Kokutai, Sasebo Naval Air Base, 1922
The F.5 was the IJNAF's first flying boat. Production in Japan began at the Yokosuka Kaigun Kosho in 1921, shifting to the Hiro Kaigun Kosho at the end of the year. The F.5 equipped Yokosuka and Sasebo Kaigun Kokutai, serving with these units until 1930. On 3 October 1922 this aircraft, with Sub Lt Hayabara as pilot, departed from Sasebo in company with aircraft S-42 on a flight to Port Arthur (now Dalien) in China.

2
H1H1 ∃-52 (Yo-52), Yokosuka Kokutai, Yokosuka Naval Air Base, 1929
The Hiro Kaigun Kosho developed the Type 15 Flying Boat as a replacement for the F.5. The Type 15-1 (H1H1) entered service in February 1929 with Yokosuka and Sasebo Kokutai. The katakana symbol '∃', or 'Yo', on the flying boat's fuselage and rudder indicated its assignment to the Yokosuka base. On 20 May 1929,

Lt Cdr Akira Ito led two Yokosuka Kokutai Type 15 Flying Boats on a flight from Yokosuka to Saipan, stopping at Chichi Jima along the way. The round-trip covered 2455 miles, and it was the longest ocean flight the IJNAF had attempted up to that time.

3
H2H1 ∃-50 (Yo-50), Yokosuka Kokutai, Yokosuka Naval Air Base, 1933
The Type 89 (H2H1), designed at the Hiro Kaigun Kosho, was the last twin-engined biplane flying boat built for the IJNAF. The aircraft featured an all-metal hull and metal structure wings with fabric covering. The Hiro Kaigun Kosho and Kawanishi built 13 H2H1s that served from 1930 until the outbreak of the Sino-Japanese conflict in 1937.

4
H4H1 タ-38 (Ta-38), Tateyama Kokutai, Tateyama Naval Air Base, 1934
The Type 91 (H4H1) all-metal monoplane flying boat was intended

as a replacement for the Type 15 and Type 89 Flying Boats. The Hiro Kaigun Kosho built around 30 H4H1s, with Kawanishi constructing an additional 17. The katakana symbol '夕', or 'Ta', on the aircraft's fuselage and tail stood for Tateyama, identifying the flying boat's assignment to the Tateyama base. Tateyama Kokutai used the H4H1 to perform long-distance flights between Japan and the Bonin Islands and Formosa. In the early stages of the Sino-Japanese conflict, small numbers of H4H1s flew patrols along the coast of China and transported cargo between China and Japan.

5
H6K2 ヨ八-37 (Yo Ha-37), Yokohama Kokutai, Yokohama Naval Air Base, 1939

As the IJNAF's first dedicated flying boat unit, Yokohama Kokutai was an early recipient of the new Type 97 (H6K) – this example was assigned to it in 1939. Yokohama Kokutai initially marked its flying boats with the Katakana 'ヨ八' code, 'Yo Ha' being an abbreviation for Yokohama. In November 1940 the unit adopted a simple Roman letter 'Y', followed by the aircraft number. At this time the IJNAF's flying boats had an all-metal finish.

6
H6K4 O-10, Toko Kokutai, Ambon, Netherlands East Indies, January–February 1942

A few months after the Pacific War began, the IJNAF changed the camouflage scheme for flying boats from overall light grey to IJN Dark Green over IJN Light Grey, but all-metal H6K4s remained on operations well into 1942. Toko Kokutai used the Roman letter 'O' as its identifier following the unit's formation as the IJNAF's second dedicated flying boat unit. This side view is a representation of what a Toko Kokutai H6K4 would have looked like in the early months of the Pacific War.

7
H6K4 W-40, 14th Kokutai, Jaluit Atoll, May 1942

Activated in April 1942, 14th Kokutai took over responsibility for patrolling the Central Pacific from Yokohama Kokutai as the latter unit was drawn deeper into the conflict in the South Pacific. The air group used the identifier 'W' from April to November 1942.

8
H6K4 Y-44, Yokohama Kokutai, Rabaul, July 1942

Yokohama Kokutai used the Roman letter 'Y' as its identifier from November 1940 through to the November 1942 reorganisation of IJNAF land-based units. Until its near annihilation in August 1942, Yokohama Kokutai operated H6K4s, by then in the standard Dark Green and Light Grey scheme seen here, from Rabaul and the Shortland Islands south of Bougainville.

9
H6K5 O-46, Toko Kokutai, Shortland Islands, October 1942

Kawanishi began building H6K5s in late 1942, this variant of the 'Mavis' introducing more powerful Mitsubishi Kinsei 53 engines that each produced 1300 hp for take-off. This gave the H6K5 higher maximum and cruising speeds but slightly less range than the H6K4. Kawanishi also added a stowable 7.7mm machine gun just behind the cockpit. Following heavy losses suffered by Yokohama Kokutai, Toko Kokutai shifted to Rabaul and the Shortland Islands in August 1942.

10
H6K4 U3-30, 801st Kokutai, Horomushiro Naval Air Base, 1943

In the reorganisation of November 1942, Yokohama Kokutai became 801st Kokutai. Having been withdrawn to Japan following losses in the Solomons, the Kokutai changed its identifier to 'U3' in April 1943 and used it until year-end. In 1944, the Kokutai shifted to using '801' as its identifier, applying this to its aircraft until the unit gave up flying boats at the end of April 1945. U3-30 flew out of the seaplane base at Horomushiro, on Hokkaido in northern Japan.

11
H6K5 N1-42, 802nd Kokutai, Jaluit, 1943

Formerly 14th Kokutai, 802nd Kokutai used the identifier 'W' for just three months, from November 1942 until January 1943, when the unit changed to 'N1' as seen here. This was retained until August 1943, when 802nd Kokutai switched to '802' – an identifier it retained until disbandment in April 1944. This particular H6K5 likely flew from one of the Kokutai's Central Pacific bases during the early months of 1943.

12
H6K5 タク-66, Takuma Kokutai, Takuma Naval Air Base, 1944

Takuma Kokutai was formed on 1 June 1943 at the IJNAF seaplane base at Takuma to train flying boat crews. The unit had on strength the Aichi Navy Type 2 Training Flying Boat (H9A1) and several H6K4/5s and H8K2s for transition training. On 25 April 1945, Takuma Kokutai gave up its training role and became a frontline unit, consolidating all the flying boats that remained operational with 801st Kokutai.

13
H6K5 KEA-83, 901st Kokutai, Toko, Formosa, early 1944

Activated in December 1943, 901st Kokutai operated H6K4/5s on convoy escort and ASW patrols from bases in the Pacific, on Formosa and in Southeast Asia. During 1944, the Kokutai equipped some of its H6Ks with MAD devices. 901st Kokutai used 'KEA' as an identifier, followed by an individual number for the aircraft. 'KE' denoted assignment to the Grand Escort Headquarters, while 'A' identified 901st Kokutai.

14
H6K4-L P-922, Eleventh Koku Kantai, 1943

At the IJNAF's request, Kawanishi built 20 H6K4-L transports in 1942–43. Featuring increased tankage and devoid of armament, they were assigned to the transport units at Koku Kantai and Koku Sentai, serving as staff transports and ferrying equipment between the IJN's far-flung bases. This example served with Eleventh Koku Kantai during 1943.

15
13-Shi Ogata Hiko Tei second prototype, Naruo, January 1941

After test flights in January 1941, the 13-Shi Ogata Hiko Tei prototype was delivered to the IJNAF on 26 March 1941. Further trials resulted in modifications to the second prototype, depicted here, including an extended nose to incorporate a gun turret and longitudinal strips on the lower hull beneath the cockpit to prevent spray from damaging the propellers. In 1943 Kawanishi converted all three 13-Shi prototypes into transports by adding compartments for 41 passengers. These aircraft became the basis for the H8K2-L Seiku (Clear Sky) transport version of the 'Emily'.

16
H8K1 Y-71, Yokohama Kokutai, Jaluit Atoll, February 1942
This aircraft, which was just the third production example of the H8K1 built by Kawanishi, was assigned to Yokohama Kokutai along with the fifth production aircraft for the second raid on Pearl Harbor. Given the tail number Y-71, the flying boat had IJN Dark Green applied to the wing uppersurfaces and the sides of the fuselage just prior to the long-range mission. Following the failed Pearl Harbor operation on the night of 3 March 1942, Lt Hisao Hashizume and his crew undertook a reconnaissance flight to Midway Island one week later. The flying boat was intercepted by F2A-3 fighters from VMF-221 and shot down.

17
H8K1 W-45, 14th Kokutai, Rabaul, July 1942
In May 1942 14th Kokutai received several early-build H8K1s, including the aircraft depicted here. Coded W-45, it was one of two Type 2s that bombed Townsville on the night of 25 July 1942. After Yokosuka Kokutai suffered heavy losses around Guadalcanal, 14th Kokutai sent several flying boats to Rabaul and the Shortland Islands to bolster long-range reconnaissance. On 27 August, while W-45 was operating from the Shortland Islands, F4F-4s from VF-71 embarked in *Wasp* shot the flying boat down. It was the second 14th Kokutai 'Emily' to be lost in two days.

18
H8K2 801-77, 801st Kokutai, Yokohama Naval Air Base, October 1944
In 1944 801st Kokutai switched its identifier to '801', plus the individual aircraft number. This late-production H8K2 featured airborne search radar Yagi antennas on either side of the nose and flat sliding hatches replacing the gun blisters on the fuselage sides just below the wings' trailing edges for additional 20 mm cannon. Based at Yokohama, 801st Kokutai flew patrols out over the approaches to the home islands. While on one such mission on 31 October 1944, 801-77 encountered a PB4Y-1 from VB-117 several hundred miles east of Okinawa and was shot down.

19
H8K2 N1-26, 802nd Kokutai, Saipan, early 1944
Illustrated here in the markings the 'Emily' wore when it initially entered service, this aircraft is the sole surviving IJNAF flying boat from World War 2. Built at Kawanishi's Konan factory, probably in March 1943, it was initially allocated to 802nd Kokutai and assigned the identifier N1-26. The aircraft likely flew patrols in the Central Pacific. When 802nd Kokutai was disbanded in April 1944, the 'Emily' was transferred to 801st Kokutai and renumbered 801-86. It flew with the unit for a year until 801st Kokutai was disbanded, after which the 'Emily' joined Takuma Kokutai and became T-31. Following its capture shortly after war's end, the flying boat was shipped by the US Navy to NAS Patuxent River for tests. Remarkably, it was preserved, and eventually returned to Japan in 1979. Carefully restored, it now resides at the Kanoya Air Base Museum in Kagoshima.

20
H8K2 51-085, 851st Kokutai, Palau, June 1944
851st Kokutai used the identifier '51-' or '851-' from the end of 1943 until the unit was disbanded in September 1944. Three months prior to its disbandment following heavy losses in and around the Marianas, 851st Kokutai was ordered to advance from its base at Davao to Palau. While flying southwest of Palau, possibly on its way back to Davao on 2 July 1944, this search radar-equipped flying boat was intercepted by a patrolling PB4Y-1 from VB-115 and shot down.

21
H8K2 KEA-03, 901st Kokutai, Yokosuka Naval Air Base, July–August 1944
In the summer of 1944 901st Kokutai acquired several H8K2s and used them alongside H6K4/5s on convoy escort patrols. In a highly unusual move for a flying boat-equipped unit, 901st Kokutai marked both types with a diagonal red stripe, bordered in white, on the fin/rudder assembly. In April 1945 all remaining 901st Kokutai flying boats were transferred to Takuma Kokutai.

22
H8K2-L Seiku 21-07, 1021st Kokutai, Yokosuka Naval Air Base, July–August 1944
1021st Kokutai, formed in January 1944, was one of several dedicated transport units formed by the IJNAF and equipped with both flying boats and land-based G4M 'Betty' bombers. Kawanishi built 36 H8K2-L transports in 1943–45 to replace the earlier H6K4-L. 1021st Kokutai used '21-' as a unit identifier, followed by the aeroplane number. In July 1945, 1021st Kokutai was absorbed into fellow transport unit 1081st Kokutai and gave up its flying boats.

23
H8K2 801-904, 801st Kokutai, Takuma Naval Air Base, March 1945
One of the last significant missions for 801st Kokutai was its participation in Operation *Tan No 2* – the attack by Azusa Tokubetsu Kogekitai on the US Navy anchorage at Ulithi Atoll. This aircraft acted as one of the pathfinders that led the two formations of P1Y1 'Frances' medium bombers in the direction of Ulithi. One of the H8K2 pathfinders was shot down by a patrolling PB4Y-1 and a second 'Emily' crash-landed on an island in the Carolines.

24
H8K2 T-28, Takuma Kokutai, Takuma Naval Air Base, April 1945
Takuma Kokutai was the IJNAF's last dedicated flying boat unit. Having acquired late-production H8K2s from 801st and 901st Kokutai, as illustrated here, Takuma Kokutai used the aircraft in scouting patrols as crews searched for US Navy task forces in the seas to the southeast of Kyushu towards Okinawa. Takuma Kokutai shared the mission with 801st Kokutai, which, having given up its flying boats, was equipped with G4M 'Betty' bombers.

INDEX

Page locators in **bold** refer to illustrations. Colour plate locators are marked 'cp.', with page locators for plate and commentary in brackets.